WILDLY
CREATIVE
PUZZLES
WITH A POINT

BY ALI THOMPSON

Group
Loveland, Colorado
group.com

Group resources really work!

This Group resource incorporates our R.E.A.L. approach to ministry. It reinforces a growing friendship with Jesus, encourages long-term learning, and results in life transformation, because it's

Relational
Learner-to-learner interaction enhances learning and builds Christian friendships.

Experiential
What learners experience through discussion and action sticks with them up to 9 times longer than what they simply hear or read.

Applicable
The aim of Christian education is to equip learners to be both hearers and doers of God's Word.

Learner-based
Learners understand and retain more when the learning process takes into consideration how they learn best.

CREDITS
Author: Ali Thompson
Executive Editor: Christine Yount Jones
Editor: Scott Firestone IV
Copy Editor: Becky Helzer
Senior Art Director: Rebecca Swain
Book Designer: Jean Bruns
Design Team: Amber Gomez Balanzar, Kate Elvin, Suzi Jensen
Maze Puzzle Developer: Julie K. Cohen / www.juliekcohen.com
Illustrator: Matt Wood

Unless otherwise indicated, all Scripture quotations are taken from the *Holy Bible*, New Living Translation, copyright © 1996, 2004, 2007, 2013. Used by permission of Tyndale House Publishers, Inc., Carol Stream, Illinois 60188. All rights reserved.

ISBN 978-1-4707-1887-9
10 9 8 7 6 5 4 3 2 1   19 18 17 16 15
Printed in the United States of America.

WILDLY CREATIVE PUZZLES WITH A POINT

CONTENTS

THE PUZZLES!

ANSWER KEY!

WILDLY CREATIVE PUZZLES WITH A POINT

INTRODUCTION

Kids learn in different ways. Some learn best by moving, others by drawing, and others by reading. Puzzles can be a powerful learning tool for the child who learns best through logic.

Unfortunately, puzzles are often misused as time-fillers and are not used as learning tools. It's easy to make a quick copy of a word search and leave kids with the busywork of finding hidden words if you need to fill a few minutes.

This book takes the busywork out of puzzles and gives them a point. Kids won't be doing puzzles just to fill time; they'll be doing them to learn more about God's Word and how to live out their faith. Each puzzle in this book is tied to a Bible passage and can be added to a lesson to help kids dig deeper into the topic. Here's what makes *Wildly Creative Puzzles With a Point* a great resource for your ministry.

The pages in this book are reproducible, so no matter how many kids you have, you can include everyone in the learning.

Each puzzle is based on a Bible passage, which makes it easy for you to tie it to a lesson. In the indexes, puzzles are ordered by the books of the Bible, so finding the puzzle you need for a lesson about Noah is easy!

Each puzzle emphasizes at least two faith-building themes. The puzzles are all labeled with faith-building themes so leaders are equipped to help kids understand the point. There's also an index listing puzzles by faith-building theme so you can quickly find a puzzle on a particular topic.

The puzzles are used as object lessons to help kids understand their faith. Each puzzle begins with an explanation of what makes it unique. No more word searches just for the sake of finding meaningless words. With this book, the puzzles themselves become an experience that helps kids dive into their faith.

There's a lot of variety. Your kids won't get bored doing crossword puzzle after crossword puzzle. Throughout this book, you'll find 41 different types of puzzles. That leaves very few repeats! Kids will love new and fresh experiences each time you use a puzzle from this book.

Each puzzle leads to discussion. As with any experience, learning is best cemented when kids can talk about it and make discoveries. We've provided great thought-provoking questions that will help kids unpack the meaning behind each puzzle.

Each puzzle is accompanied by leader instructions. These easy-to-follow, step-by-step instructions equip leaders to make sure each puzzle truly is an experience—not busywork.

This book can be used for a variety of ages. Each puzzle is labeled with recommended ages and created to be just right for those ages. Check out the age-level index to choose a puzzle that's just right for your group of kids.

Families are involved, too! Each puzzle page includes a set of questions for kids to talk about with their families. Parents will know that their kids aren't doing puzzles as time-fillers and that you're intentionally using every moment with their kids to help them grow in their relationships with Jesus.

Now you no longer have to fear those times when the sermon runs long and you're not sure when parents are arriving. Simply grab this book, look up the puzzle that fits with your lesson, and lead kids through an amazing experience that will help them grow in their faith.

PUZZLES WITH A POINT SUPPLIES

One great feature of this book is that it's relatively supply-free. However, in addition to a Bible, you'll want to have these supplies on hand for some of the puzzles:

* pencils
* pens
* crayons
* markers
* scissors
* tape
* highlighters

THIS WAY TO THE WILDLY CREATIVE PUZZLES WITH A POINT

GOD CREATES THE WORLD

Genesis 1

Creation,
God's power

Connect-the-dot puzzles are common for preschool kids. But this puzzle is more than meets the eye. The discussion that follows will help kids discover how God made the world. Don't miss the importance of discussing this puzzle with your preschoolers.

WHAT YOU'LL DO

1. Make a photocopy of the puzzle page for each child. Help kids write their names on it.

2. Have kids connect the dots, using pencils, by following the numbers on the first three pictures. Younger preschoolers may need assistance, so be ready to help as needed.

3. Lead kids in this discussion:

- **How did you know what to do to make your picture?**

4. Have kids tightly close their eyes and try to connect the dots on the fourth picture. Then ask:

- **What was harder about making your last picture?**

5. Read aloud Genesis 1:3, 9, and 24, and lead kids in this discussion:

- **What did God do to make the world?**

- **How did God know what to make when there wasn't anything in the world yet?**

- **You made some pictures with your eyes open and one with your eyes closed. Which do you think is more like the way God made the world? Why?**

6. Say: **You did a great job making pictures by connecting the dots. But when God made the world, there were no dots for him to connect. He made the world out of nothing! It was kind of like when you tried to connect the dots without being able to see. But God's creation came out perfectly, even though he didn't have anything to help him make it. God is very creative, and we can show we love him by taking care of the things he made.**

7. Send the papers home with kids so they can talk with their families about the questions on their puzzle.

SOLUTION
SHOWN ON
PAGE 115

GOD CREATES THE WORLD

Genesis 1

Connect the dots in order for the first three pictures. For the last picture, try it with your eyes closed!

1

2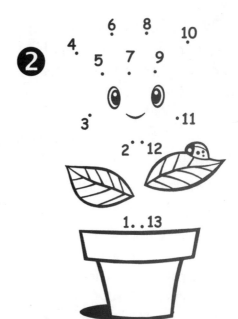

3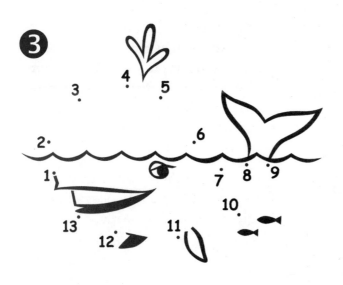

4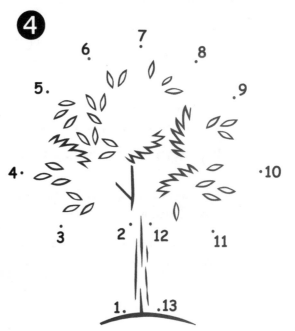

TALK With Your Family

▶ Which picture is your favorite? Why?

▶ What's something God made that you really like to take care of?

YOU ARE SPECIAL

made in God's image, identity

Genesis 1:26-28; Psalm 139

Kids often feel as if they aren't very special. They may be acutely aware of the ways they're different from others, but that awareness may make them feel more weird than special. This puzzle is more than a traditional "spot the differences" puzzle because the discussion that follows can help kids understand why God values them—differences and all.

WHAT YOU'LL DO

1. Make a photocopy of the puzzle page for each child. Have kids write their names on it.

2. Tell kids to circle the six differences between the two pictures. If some kids are having a hard time finding them all, make sure they don't feel ashamed or as if they've failed. Have kids who finish early provide clues to help others finish, if needed. If all the kids are stuck, use the solutions page to help give clues.

3. Lead kids in this discussion:

- **What differences did you notice between the two pictures?**

- **What differences have you noticed between yourself and other people?**

- **In what ways are all people alike?**

4. Read aloud Genesis 1:26-28, and lead kids in this discussion:

- **If God made us in his image, why is everyone different?**

5. Read aloud Psalm 139:13-14, and lead kids in this discussion:

- **What are some things that make you special and show that God made you wonderfully?**

If you know the kids well, share some of your own observations about the things that make them special.

6. Say: **God gave us all similarities and differences—and he did that on purpose! The things that make you different from others can show a different side of who God is because we're all made in his image. God made *you* wonderfully, and he thinks you're special!**

7. Send the papers home with kids so they can talk with their families about the questions on their puzzle.

SOLUTION
SHOWN ON
PAGE 115

YOU ARE SPECIAL

Genesis 1:26-28;
Psalm 139

Find the six differences between these two pictures.

TALK
With Your Family

▸ What makes each of us different from one another?

▸ Why might God consider those things special?

ADAM AND EVE'S BAD CHOICE

Genesis 3

temptation, sin

Mazes are a blast for elementary kids! But this is no ordinary maze. This maze will show them the consequences of making wrong decisions—and the discussion that follows will help them know how to **make better choices.**

WHAT YOU'LL DO

1. Make a photocopy of the puzzle page for each child. Have kids write their names on it.

2. Have kids try to complete the maze using pens.

3. Lead kids in this discussion:

- **Did you make any wrong turns? If so, what was that like? If not, how did you avoid making any wrong turns?**

- **Tell about a time you made a "wrong turn" in your life. What were the consequences?**

4. Read aloud Genesis 3:16-19, and lead kids in this discussion:

- **What do you think about the consequences of Adam and Eve's bad choices?**

- **How do those consequences still affect us today?**

- **What can you learn from Adam and Eve's mistakes?**

5. Say: **Any mistakes you made on your paper are there to stay because you used a pen to complete your maze. When we make sinful choices, sometimes the consequences are like that ink: they don't go away. But the good news is, Jesus forgives our sins if we believe in him. Jesus helps us learn how to make better choices.**

6. Send the papers home with kids so they can talk with their families about the questions on their puzzle.

SOLUTION
SHOWN ON
PAGE 116

WILDLY CREATIVE PUZZLES WITH A POINT

ADAM AND EVE'S BAD CHOICE

 Genesis 3

Use a pen to complete the maze below. Try not to end up in any sinful spots!

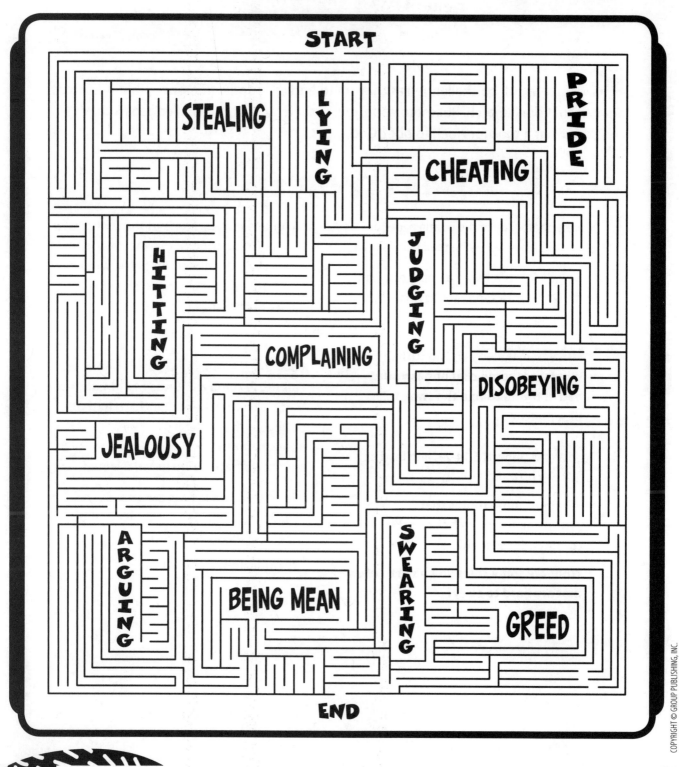

START

STEALING LYING PRIDE
CHEATING
HITTING JUDGING
COMPLAINING
DISOBEYING
JEALOUSY
ARGUING BEING MEAN SWEARING GREED

END

TALK
With Your Family

▶ What are some choices you know are wrong but are tempted to make anyway?

▶ What can help you make choices that honor God?

13

NOAH AND THE FLOOD

Genesis 6–9

obedience,
God's commands

Kids' minds will be challenged as they try to find the subtle differences that rule out the animals that don't match. But more importantly, their faith will be challenged as they consider what it took for Noah to obey God.

WHAT YOU'LL DO

1. Make a photocopy of the puzzle page for each child. Have kids write their names on it.

2. Have kids find the two matching elephants and the two matching rabbits on their puzzle pages.

3. Lead kids in this discussion:

- **What were some challenges you had in trying to find the two that matched?**

4. Read aloud Genesis 6:14-21, and lead kids in this discussion:

- **What are some things that sound challenging about God's commands to Noah?**

- **What are some rules you have to obey that are hard to obey?**

- **In our puzzle, some of the pictures may have tried to distract you from finding the matching pairs. What are some things that can distract you from obeying?**

5. Say: **It's a good thing Noah obeyed God! Because he obeyed God, his family and all those different kinds of animals were safe during the flood. If Noah had disobeyed, the world would've ended! It's important that we obey God, too, even when it's hard or we get distracted.**

6. Send the papers home with kids so they can talk with their families about the questions on their puzzle.

SOLUTION
SHOWN ON
PAGE 116

NOAH AND THE FLOOD

Genesis 6-9

Noah had to find pairs of animals. Now it's your turn! Two elephants are an exact match. Which two are they? When you find them, move on and find the two rabbits that are an exact match.

A

B

A   B

C

D

C   D

E

F

E   F

TALK
With Your Family

▶ **Why is it important that Noah obeyed God?**

▶ **What's one way you want to obey God this week?**

JOSEPH'S RAINBOW COAT

obedience, good choices

Genesis 37

It can be hard for preschoolers to understand cause and effect. They're just beginning to learn that certain behaviors result in certain rewards or punishments. This puzzle will give preschoolers a visual, concrete way to see how one thing can lead to another.

WHAT YOU'LL DO

1. Make a photocopy of the puzzle page for each child. Help kids write their names on it.

2. Have kids determine which Joseph is connected to which location.

3. Lead kids in this discussion:

- **What are some of the different places Joseph went in our puzzle?**

4. Read aloud Genesis 37:3-7, and lead kids in this discussion:

- **Tell about a time you heard someone brag. What did you do?**

- **What can happen when you brag?**

5. Read aloud Genesis 41-43, and lead kids in this discussion:

- **Tell about a time you obeyed and something good happened to you.**

- **What good things can happen when we obey?**

6. Say: **Joseph made a lot of different choices. At first he made a choice to brag to his brothers, and they sent him away. But after that, he decided to obey God over and over and over. And when Joseph obeyed, God brought him to good places. He ultimately became a helper for the king! Joseph didn't know if good things would happen when he obeyed, but he obeyed anyway. And God wants us to obey even when we don't know how things will end up.**

7. Send the papers home with kids so they can talk with their families about the questions on their puzzle.

SOLUTION SHOWN ON PAGE 117

16

JOSEPH'S RAINBOW COAT

Genesis 37

In the Bible, Joseph went to a lot of different places! Which Joseph connects to which place?

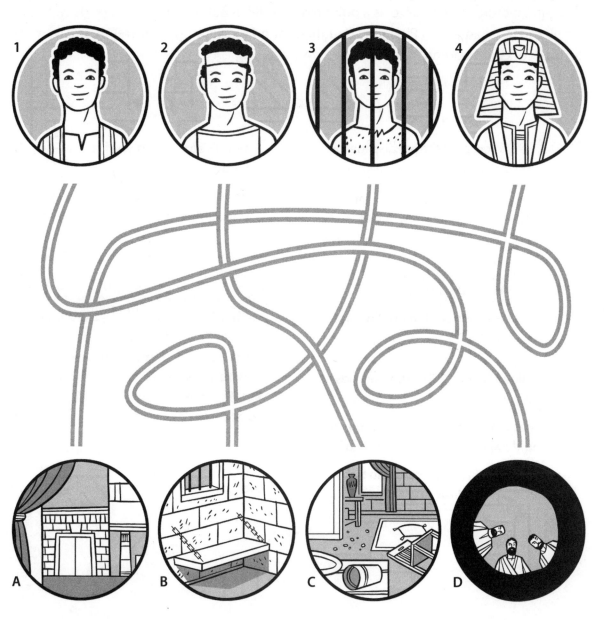

TALK
With Your Family

▶ What are some bad things that can happen when we make bad choices? What are some good things that can happen when we make good choices?

▶ How does God help us obey even when it's difficult?

OK TO COPY

GOD PROTECTS BABY MOSES

Exodus 2:1-10

God's plan,
God's leading

Finding pictures can be used as a pointless time-filler. But not in this case! Kids will use this puzzle to explore how Pharaoh's daughter found Moses among the reeds and how they can look for God's leading in their lives.

WHAT YOU'LL DO

1. Make a photocopy of the puzzle page for each child. Have kids write their names on it.

2. Have kids try to find the following items hidden within the picture: a basket, 10 reeds, a crown, baby Moses, Moses' sister, the letter "M" for Moses. Allow time.

3. Lead kids in this discussion:

- **What was your strategy to find the items quickly?**

4. Read aloud Exodus 2:1-6, and lead kids in this discussion:

- **What are some dangerous things that could happen to a baby in a river?**

- **God helped the princess find baby Moses. What does that tell you about God?**

- **What's something you've felt God leading you to do?**

- **What can you do to look for ways God is leading you?**

5. Say: **The Egyptian princess didn't even know God, but he led her to find Moses and save him. God even worked it out so that Moses got to go back to his mom for a while! God has a plan even when we can't see it. Sometimes we need to look to see what God's plan for us is. But if we look for his plan, he'll show us what to do.**

6. Send the papers home with kids so they can talk with their families about the questions on their puzzle.

SOLUTION
SHOWN ON
PAGE 117

GOD PROTECTS BABY MOSES

Exodus 2:1-10

Find the following items hidden within the picture:

- ☐ a basket
- ☐ 10 reeds
- ☐ a crown
- ☐ baby Moses
- ☐ Moses' sister
- ☐ the letter "M" for Moses

TALK
With Your Family

▶ What are some ways God can show people what to do?

▶ What's one way you want to look for God's plan in your life?

MOSES AND THE BURNING BUSH

Exodus 3:1-10

God's messages, hearing from God

This word search is far more than just circling words. It will help upper-elementary kids look for God in the midst of the ordinary. This puzzle will open up a great dialogue about what messages God has for kids today.

WHAT YOU'LL DO

1. Make a photocopy of the puzzle page for each child. Have kids write their names on it.

2. Have kids use highlighters to find the words listed in the puzzle. Then have kids take note of the leftover letters and write them in order to spell out a special message.

3. Lead kids in this discussion:

- **If you didn't have all the ordinary words to find first, how would you have found the hidden message?**

- **In what ways have you heard or seen a message from God hidden in the midst of ordinary things?**

4. Read aloud Exodus 3:1-10, and lead kids in this discussion:

- **What was ordinary about Moses' actions in this passage? What was extraordinary?**

- **How might God be trying to get your attention right now?**

5. Say: **Moses was going about an ordinary day, tending his sheep and walking past a bush, when something extraordinary happened. Moses could've been in such a hurry that he walked on by. But instead he stopped and received a message from God. Let's take time in our ordinary lives to watch and listen for the messages God is sending to us.**

6. Have kids take a few moments of silence to listen to God.

7. Send the papers home with kids so they can talk with their families about the questions on their puzzle.

SOLUTION
SHOWN ON
PAGE 117

MOSES AND THE BURNING BUSH

Exodus 3:1-10

Find the words in bold below from Exodus 3:1-10 hidden in the word search.

• • • • • • • • • • • • • • • • • •

One day **Moses** was tending the flock of his father-in-law, Jethro, the priest of Midian. He led the **flock** far into the wilderness and came to **Sinai**, the mountain of God. There the **angel** of the Lord appeared to him in a blazing **fire** from the middle of a **bush**. Moses stared in amazement. Though the bush was **engulfed** in **flames**, it didn't burn up. "This is amazing," Moses said to himself. "Why isn't that bush burning up? I must go see it."

When the **Lord** saw Moses coming to take a closer look, God **called** to him from the middle of the bush, "Moses! Moses!"

"Here I am!" Moses replied.

"Do not come any closer," the Lord warned. "Take off your sandals, for you are standing on holy **ground**. I am the **God** of your father—the God of Abraham, the God of Isaac, and the God of Jacob." When Moses heard this, he covered his face because he was afraid to look at God.

Then the Lord told him, "I have certainly seen the **oppression** of my people in Egypt. I have heard their cries of distress because of their harsh slave drivers. Yes, I am aware of their suffering. So I have come down to **rescue** them from the power of the Egyptians and lead them out of Egypt into their own fertile and spacious land. It is a land flowing with milk and honey—the land where the Canaanites, Hittites, Amorites, Perizzites, Hivites, and Jebusites now live. Look! The **cry** of the people of Israel has reached me, and I have seen how harshly the Egyptians abuse them. Now go, for I am **sending** you to Pharaoh. You must **lead** my people Israel out of Egypt."

G	I	A	N	I	S	O	D	D	I
S	D	N	U	O	R	G	O	F	S
M	C	L	E	A	D	A	G	L	E
O	P	P	R	E	S	S	I	O	N
S	E	B	U	S	H	Y	R	C	D
E	R	L	A	N	G	E	L	K	I
S	I	L	C	A	L	L	E	D	N
I	F	L	A	M	E	S	N	R	G
D	E	F	L	U	G	N	E	O	G
Y	R	E	S	C	U	E	O	L	U

NOW WRITE THE LEFTOVER LETTERS IN ORDER TO SPELL A SECRET MESSAGE:

___ ___ ___ ___   ___ ___ ___ ___ ___ ___ ___   ___ ___   ___ ___ ___ ___ ___ ___ ___ ___ ___ ___ ___ ___ ___ ___ .

TALK
With Your Family

▶ **Describe an ordinary day in your life. When has God sent you a message during an ordinary time?**

▶ **What can you do to look and listen for God in the midst of ordinary things?**

THE TEN PLAGUES

Exodus 7–12

God's power, hard times

Many kids learn through images. A memorable picture can cement a Bible event in kids' minds. As kids look for the pictures hidden throughout this puzzle, they'll get a clear image of just how much the plagues took over Egypt, and they'll explore God's power in their own lives.

WHAT YOU'LL DO

1. Make a photocopy of the puzzle page for each child. Have kids write their names on it.

2. Have kids try to find five items for each of the five plagues represented. Because this will be a total of 25 items, you may need to cut the time short before everyone finishes. If that's the case, have kids share answers to see if they can find every item.

3. Read aloud Exodus 7:1-5, and say: **After God said this, he did just what he said he'd do. He sent 10 awful plagues that took over Egypt. You saw some of those in your picture.** Lead kids in this discussion:

- **Of all the plagues you saw in the picture or the other ones you know about, which seems the worst to you? Explain.**

- **Which plague do you think most shows God's power? Explain.**

- **What's something that feels like a plague to you right now—a problem that seems as if it's taking over your life?**

- **What are some ways you'd like to see God's power over that "plague"?**

4. Say: **The plagues were really awful. But they came from God to teach the Egyptians a lesson. God even kept the Israelites, his people, safe from many of the plagues. His power is amazing! And that same power is available for us to use when we face hard times.**

5. Send the papers home with kids so they can talk with their families about the questions on their puzzle.

SOLUTION
SHOWN ON
PAGE 118

THE TEN PLAGUES

Exodus 7–12

Good sent 10 plagues to Egypt. Can you find five of each item for the five plagues listed?

LOCUSTS

FROGS

FLIES

LIVESTOCK

LIGHTNING

TALK
With Your Family

▶ How have you seen God's power?

▶ What are some ways you'd like to see God's power take over your life?

GOD PARTS THE RED SEA

God's timing, trusting God

Exodus 14:1-29

Each of the words in this puzzle has been carefully chosen to help kids consider God's power and timing. As kids do this puzzle, they'll talk about the words they connect to give meaning and insight to the passage.

WHAT YOU'LL DO

1. Make a photocopy of the puzzle page for each child. Fold the pages in half vertically, and give some kids a page with the left side facing up and others a page with the right side facing up. Have kids write their names on it, and instruct kids not to peek at the other side of their papers.

2. Read aloud Exodus 14:21-22.

3. Say: **When I say "go," you'll find a partner who has the opposite side of the page as you. When everyone has a partner, find one set of letters from each side that can be connected to make a whole word. When you've chosen your set, talk about how that word connects to our Bible passage.** Allow a minute or two for kids to find partners and discuss. Then continue four more times until kids have all connected all of the words.

4. Lead kids in this discussion:

- **Which word most stands out to you in relation to your own life?**

- **In what ways was God's timing key to this event in the Bible?**

- **When has it been hard for you to wait for God's timing?**

- **What role did trust play in this Bible passage? What about in your own life?**

5. Say: **Looking back at this passage, we can see that God had a perfect plan to get the Israelites safely away from the Egyptians. But just before God parted the Red Sea—when the Israelites were trapped between a big body of water and a powerful army—God's timing might not have seemed so great. The Israelites complained to Moses that they were going to die! We don't always understand God's timing, but we can trust him no matter what.**

6. Send the papers home with kids so they can talk with their families about the questions on their puzzle.

SOLUTION
SHOWN ON
PAGE 118

GOD PARTS THE RED SEA

Exodus 14:1-29

Through Moses, God parted the Red Sea. But the words below got caught up and split, too! Work with a partner to find the halves of words that go together.

Through Moses, God parted the Red Sea. But the words below got caught up and split, too! Work with a partner to find the halves of words that go together.

POW

TIM

SA

MI

TR

FETY

ER

UST

ING

GHTY

TALK
With Your Family

▶ What's an area of your life where you're waiting on God's timing?

▶ How can you trust God while you wait?

THE TEN COMMANDMENTS

Exodus 20

God's rules, obedience

It may be tempting to use this puzzle simply to make sure kids have a rote knowledge of the Ten Commandments. But the debriefing questions are the key to making this puzzle about understanding, not just knowledge. Don't skip over them!

WHAT YOU'LL DO

1. Make a photocopy of the puzzle page for each child. Have kids write their names on it.

2. Have kids circle the commands they think come from the Ten Commandments, put a star by the ones they think come from other places in the Bible, and cross out the ones they don't think come from the Bible. Review the answers with kids.

3. Lead kids in this discussion:

- **How did you figure out which commands were from God?**

- **What's significant about the rules that are part of the Ten Commandments?**

- **How do you know how to obey God?**

4. Read aloud Exodus 20:1-2. Lead kids in this discussion:

- **Why do you think God said who he was before he gave the Ten Commandments? What does that mean?**

- **Which of the Ten Commandments is the easiest for you to obey? the hardest?**

- **What's one way you'd like to obey God this week?**

5. Say: **God gave a lot of rules in the Bible. But when the Israelites first left Egypt, he gave them this special set of rules that would help them know how to live as they went to their new home. We can never totally obey God's rules. But the closer we get to God, the better he can help us obey. When you're facing a choice and need help knowing how to obey, think about God's Ten Commandments.**

6. Send the papers home with kids so they can talk with their families about the questions on their puzzle.

SOLUTION
SHOWN ON
PAGE 118

26

THE TEN COMMANDMENTS

Exodus 20

Circle the commands you think come from the Ten Commandments, put a star by the ones you think come from other places in the Bible, and cross out the ones you don't think come from the Bible.

- LOVE YOUR NEIGHBOR
- OBEY YOUR PARENTS
- WASH YOUR HANDS BEFORE DINNER
- REST ONE DAY A WEEK
- DON'T STEAL
- LOOK BOTH WAYS BEFORE CROSSING
- DON'T BE JEALOUS
- TAKE CARE OF CREATION
- DON'T LIE
- GO TO CHURCH EVERY SUNDAY
- DON'T KILL
- RESPECT OTHER PEOPLE
- ONLY TALK TO CHRISTIANS
- DRINK PLENTY OF WATER
- PRAY FOR YOUR ENEMIES
- DON'T WORSHIP IDOLS
- PUT GOD FIRST
- RESPECT GOD'S NAME

TALK With Your Family

▶ What's so important about the Ten Commandments?

▶ What's one commandment you want to obey better? How will you do it?

OK TO COPY

JERICHO'S FALLING WALLS

relying on God, obstacles

Joshua 6

Kids this age understand obstacles. They're beginning to see real obstacles that can make it difficult to live out their faith. This puzzle will help upper-elementary kids rely on God to cut out the obstacles in their lives so they can experience his peace, joy, and hope.

WHAT YOU'LL DO

1. Make a photocopy of the puzzle page for each child. Have kids write their names on it.

2. Have kids cross out the Ks, Qs, and Ws to reveal the words that show what God wants for our lives.

3. Lead kids in this discussion:

- **In what ways have you experienced one of the words on your paper?**

- **Based on your experiences, why are these good things God would want for us?**

4. Say: **God had hope and peace for the Israelites, too, although there'd be some battles to fight to get there. One of the first obstacles they came to when they got to their new home was a giant wall!**

5. Read aloud Joshua 6:12-14 and 20-21. Lead kids in this discussion:

- **Why was the wall an obstacle to achieving what God wanted for the Israelites?**

- **What options did the Israelites have to deal with this obstacle?**

- **What are some obstacles that can keep you from experiencing hope, joy, peace, love, or trust?**

- **How can you rely on God to help you overcome those obstacles?**

6. Say: **The Israelites could've relied on themselves and tried to break down the wall on their own. They could've not relied on *anyone* and just given up. But instead they relied on God and followed his unusual plan to knock down the wall. They marched around it for seven days and just as God said, he knocked down the wall. We can rely on God to remove the obstacles in our lives that make it harder to experience his hope and peace.**

7. Send the papers home with kids so they can talk with their families about the questions on their puzzle.

SOLUTION
SHOWN ON
PAGE 118

JERICHO'S FALLING WALLS

Joshua 6

The Israelites marched around the walls of Jericho until the walls fell down. Take out all the Ks, Qs, and Ws and see what God wants in your life.

TALK
With Your Family

▶ **Why do you believe God wants these things for you?**

▶ **What are some "walls" God needs to knock down for you to experience these things?**

RUTH STAYS WITH NAOMI

Ruth 1

Christian influence, role models

Preschoolers are just starting to learn how to match things, so they'll enjoy the challenge of matching objects that go well together in this puzzle. And in the discussion, they'll learn what kinds of behaviors "match" Christians—and how we can follow role models who will help us follow God.

WHAT YOU'LL DO

1. Make a photocopy of the puzzle page for each child. Help kids write their names on it.

2. Have kids draw lines to pair up objects that go well together.

3. Lead kids in this discussion:

- **What are some other things you can think of that go well together?**

- **How do you know if something goes well with something else?**

4. Say: **In the Bible, a woman named Ruth said she would stay with another woman, named Naomi. She wanted to follow Naomi's God—our God!**

5. Read aloud Ruth 1:16-18. Lead kids in this discussion:

- **Who are some people you like to spend time with?**

- **How can those people help you follow God?**

- **What kinds of actions seem to match well with people who love God?**

6. Say: **Ruth came from a country where people didn't know who God was. But she wanted to follow Naomi and love Naomi's God. We can stick with people who follow God so we can learn how to love and follow him better.**

7. Send the papers home with kids so they can talk with their families about the questions on their puzzle.

SOLUTION
SHOWN ON
PAGE 119

RUTH STAYS WITH NAOMI

Ruth said she'd stay with Naomi. Some things just go together really well! Draw lines between the two columns to match the things that go well together.

TALK
With Your Family

▶ What kinds of actions go well with loving God?

▶ Who are some people who can help you know how to follow God?

31

SAMUEL HEARS GOD

1 Samuel 3

understanding God's voice, hearing from God

Upper-elementary kids still think very concretely, so at times the concept of listening to God may be hard to understand. Will God speak to them audibly? After they decode this puzzle, kids will be able to grapple with the ways God speaks to people today.

WHAT YOU'LL DO

1. Make a photocopy of the puzzle page for each child. Have kids write their names on it.

2. Have kids use the decoder key to decode the puzzle. If some kids are having trouble, give them these additional clues one at a time: A = L, P = O, R = E, Y = T, and E = W.

3. Lead kids in this discussion:

- **When God speaks to us, do you think it's like a code or not? Talk about that.**

4. Read aloud 1 Samuel 3:1-10. Lead kids in this discussion:

- **How was our puzzle like or unlike the way God spoke to Samuel?**

- **Samuel didn't even know God was speaking to him at first; what do you think about that?**

- **What are some ways God can speak to people very clearly?**

- **What are some ways people might get God's messages confused?**

5. Say: **God can still speak to people today. But like Samuel, we need to listen for God's voice. Our puzzle can help us remember one way to listen for God: Be still. And the more we get to know God, the more easily we'll be able to hear his voice in our hearts.**

6. Send the papers home with kids so they can talk with their families about the questions on their puzzle.

SOLUTION
SHOWN ON
PAGE 119

SAMUEL HEARS GOD

1 Samuel 3

Decode the message from God below. Use the hints to the right to figure out some of the letters.

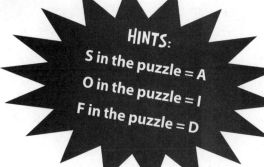

HINTS:
S in the puzzle = A
O in the puzzle = I
F in the puzzle = D

NR DYOAA, SMF LMPE

YJSY O SZ HPF!

—— ————, ——— ———— ———— — —— ——— !

BE STILL, AND KNOW THAT I AM GOD!

TALK
With Your Family

▶ What are some ways God speaks to people?

▶ What are some ways God's message could get scrambled?

OK TO COPY

SAMUEL ANOINTS DAVID

1 Samuel 16

hearts for God, growing relationship with God

Mazes are all about obstacles and misleading paths. Kids this age may think they can set up enough false pretenses to hide some of the sin in their hearts from God. But this maze and the discussion will help them understand that God looks right into their hearts.

WHAT YOU'LL DO

1. Make a photocopy of the puzzle page for each child. Have kids write their names on it.

2. Have kids start at the outside of the maze and find their way to the center.

3. Lead kids in this discussion:

- **Why was it difficult to get into the heart?**

- **How easy have you made it for God to see into your heart?**

4. Read aloud 1 Samuel 16:7. Lead kids in this discussion:

- **When God looks inside your heart, what are the good things he sees?**

What are some things you wish you could block from his view?

- **In what ways do you need to open up your heart to God more?**

5. Say: **Even when we try to hide our hearts from God, he can still see right inside. But we can make our hearts more open to God by living in a way that pleases him. God looks at our hearts, and he wants us to have hearts that show our love for him!**

6. Send the papers home with kids so they can talk with their families about the questions on their puzzle.

SOLUTION
SHOWN ON
PAGE 119

SAMUEL ANOINTS DAVID

1 Samuel 16

Complete the maze below.

START

TALK
With Your Family

▶ **What are the things God can see at the very center of your heart?**

▶ **What things would you *like* God to see at the center of your heart?**

DAVID KILLS GOLIATH

1 Samuel 17

good character, virtues

This isn't a typical word search—we haven't provided a list of words for kids to find. Instead they'll pick the first five words that stand out to them. That way, they can personalize the puzzle—and the Scripture.

WHAT YOU'LL DO

1. Make a photocopy of the puzzle page for each child. Have kids write their names on it.

2. Have kids pick the first five words they see, circle them, and then put down their pens or pencils.

3. Read aloud 1 Samuel 17:40. Lead kids in this discussion:

- **How was the way David chose his stones like or unlike the way you chose your words?**

- **Why do you think those five words stood out to you?**

4. Read aloud 1 Samuel 17:41-50. Lead kids in this discussion:

- **How did David show some of the qualities you found?**

- **What have you done to show those qualities?**

- **Why do you think it matters to have character qualities like these?**

5. Say: **Even on the battlefield, David showed character. He was brave, honest, and humble. He cared about his people and stood up to Goliath when no one else would. Most importantly, David trusted God, and God helped him win the battle! God wants us to have character like David, no matter what we're doing.**

6. Send the papers home with kids so they can talk with their families about the questions on their puzzle.

SOLUTION
SHOWN ON
PAGE 120

DAVID KILLS GOLIATH

1 Samuel 17

Circle the first five words you find in this word search, and then stop. The words you find should all be good character qualities.

K	I	N	D	N	E	S	S	P
O	C	R	H	O	P	E	F	A
G	O	L	O	V	E	L	A	T
J	U	S	T	I	C	E	I	I
B	R	A	V	E	R	Y	T	E
J	A	H	O	N	O	R	H	N
O	G	F	T	R	U	S	T	C
Y	E	P	E	A	C	E	P	E
I	N	T	E	G	R	I	T	Y

TALK
With Your Family

▶ Which character quality that you circled do you think you best show?

▶ Which qualities do you need God to help you work on?

SOLOMON ASKS FOR WISDOM

1 Kings 3

wisdom, God's plan

This word search is full of false starts that may make your kids think they've found the right word. This will lead to a great discussion about true wisdom versus the things of this world that may seem wise…but aren't.

WHAT YOU'LL DO

1. Make a photocopy of the puzzle page for each child. Have kids write their names on it.

2. Have kids search for the word *wise*. It occurs in a straight line only one time in the puzzle, but have kids count how many times they *think* they've found it and then realized it had the wrong ending.

3. Lead kids in this discussion:

- **How many times did you get tricked while you looked for the right word?**

- **When have you been fooled by a decision that seemed wise but wasn't?**

4. Read aloud 1 Kings 3:5-12. Lead kids in this discussion:

- **What can make wisdom hard to find?**

- **What does wisdom from God look like?**

- **How can you tell when you've found God's true wisdom?**

- **In what areas do you need wisdom from God right now?**

5. Say: **Solomon could've asked for anything—money, fame, popularity…you name it! But the fact that he asked for wisdom shows he already had some! Solomon knew the most important thing was turning to God for help making good choices. James 1:5 tells us we can ask God for wisdom, too. Let's do that right now.**

6. Pray with kids that God will give them wisdom and that they'll be able to distinguish it from the false wisdom the world offers. Allow some time for silent prayer so kids can pray about specific ways they need wisdom.

7. Send the papers home with kids so they can talk with their families about the questions on their puzzle.

SOLUTION
SHOWN ON
PAGE 120

38

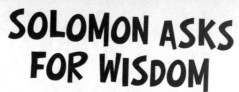

SOLOMON ASKS FOR WISDOM

1 Kings 3

Find the word *wise* in a straight line in the puzzle below. Count how many times you *think* you've found it, only to discover you didn't.

wisdom wise wiser wisely wisdom

W	I	S	W	S	I	E
I	W	E	S	I	S	W
S	W	I	E	S	W	I
W	I	S	W	I	S	I
I	S	I	S	W	E	E
E	S	I	E	I	S	W
E	E	S	E	S	E	I

TALK
With Your Family

▶ **What are some areas where you need to seek God's wisdom?**

▶ **How can you make sure you're truly finding wisdom from God?**

RAVENS FEED ELIJAH

1 Kings 17:1-6

God's provision, thankfulness

Crossword puzzles are often used to help kids remember basic facts. But this crossword puzzle does much more than help kids gain head knowledge. Instead it's a visual reminder that all their blessings come from God.

WHAT YOU'LL DO

1. Make a photocopy of the puzzle page for each child. Have kids write their names on it.

2. Have kids use the clues to fill in the crossword puzzle with blessings.

3. Lead kids in this discussion:

- **In what ways do all these blessings connect back to God?**

- **Which of these blessings are you most thankful for, and why?**

4. Read aloud 1 Kings 17:1-6. Lead kids in this discussion:

- **What kinds of blessings did God give Elijah in this passage?**

- **Why is God even more important than any of those things?**

- **What can you do to look for God in the blessings you have?**

5. Say: **Elijah needed food and water, and God gave it to him. God gives us those things, too, but sometimes we take them for granted because we're not desperate like Elijah was. We can remember that all our blessings—everything we need to survive—are gifts from God that we can be thankful for.**

6. Send the papers home with kids so they can talk with their families about the questions on their puzzle.

SOLUTION
SHOWN ON
PAGE 121

40

RAVENS FEED ELIJAH

1 Kings 17:1-6

Use the clues to fill in blessings that flow from God.

ACROSS

1. People you like to spend time with
2. Where you live
3. Things you play with
4. How you feel about your family
5. What you breathe

DOWN

1. Parents, brothers, and sisters
6. Money
7. You need to drink this
8. Pants, shirts
9. You need to eat this

TALK
With Your Family

▶ What are some things God has provided for you?

▶ How can you better recognize that these things all come from God?

ELIJAH AND THE PROPHETS OF BAAL

1 Kings 18

truth, idolatry

Word jumbles can be challenging for some kids. But that's okay! Offer them help, but recognize that the more kids are challenged by this puzzle, the better they'll understand the importance of seeking the truth.

WHAT YOU'LL DO

1. Make a photocopy of the puzzle page for each child. Have kids write their names on it.

2. Have kids unscramble the words, using 1 Kings 18 if they need help.

3. Read aloud 1 Kings 18:25-29. Lead kids in this discussion:

- **In what ways were the prophets of Baal mixed up about the truth?**

- **How was their thinking like or unlike our puzzle?**

- **What's one way you've seen people get mixed up about God?**

4. Read aloud 1 Kings 18:30-39. Lead kids in this discussion:

- **What do you think about the way Elijah straightened out the prophets of Baal?**

- **How can you keep from getting mixed up about God?**

5. Say: **The prophets of Baal had things all jumbled up. They thought Baal was a real god! But Baal was just an idol and couldn't do anything to make the sacrifice catch fire. Our God is real, though, and has the power to do anything. We can hold on to the truth about our God and avoid getting jumbled up.**

6. Send the papers home with kids so they can talk with their families about the questions on their puzzle.

SOLUTION
SHOWN ON
PAGE 121

ELIJAH AND THE PROPHETS OF BAAL 1 Kings 18

Unscramble these words. If you need help, read 1 Kings 18. All the words are in the passage!

HROGUTD

AMENIF

PPHROTSE

DROL

DNACDE

HOUTSED

TSOSNE

FEIR

TRAAL

RAETW

TALK
With Your Family

▶ Tell about someone you know who seems mixed up about the truth.

▶ How can you keep from getting mixed up?

KING JOSIAH CLEANS THE TEMPLE

2 Chronicles 34

God's Word, the Bible

Preschoolers will love looking for the hidden Bibles in this puzzle. And all their searching won't be in vain! This puzzle transitions to a wonderful conversation that will help kids understand the importance of the Bible in their lives.

WHAT YOU'LL DO

1. Make a photocopy of the puzzle page for each child. Help kids write their names on it.

2. Have kids find five Bibles hidden in the picture.

3. Lead kids in this discussion:

- **Tell about a time you lost something. What did you do to find it?**

- **Tell about a time you found something surprising.**

4. Read aloud 2 Chronicles 34:14-15, 29-32. Lead kids in this discussion:

- **Why was it important that these people found the Bible?**

- **Why is the Bible important in our lives?**

- **King Josiah read the Bible so he would know how to live. What does the Bible tell you to do?**

5. Say: **The Bible had been lost for so long that Josiah didn't even know it was missing! But it was a wonderful surprise when they found it, because the Bible is God's Word. It's a very important and special book that shows us how to live our lives. Let's look for ways to obey what the Bible tells us to do!**

6. Send the papers home with kids so they can talk with their families about the questions on their puzzle.

SOLUTION SHOWN ON PAGE 121

44

Find five Bibles hidden in this messy temple. They look like this:

KING JOSIAH CLEANS THE TEMPLE

2 Chronicles 34

TALK With Your Family

▸ What's your favorite part of the Bible?

▸ How can you take care of God's Word?

THE LORD IS MY SHEPHERD

Psalm 23

God's leading, following God

As kids move these puzzle pieces around, they'll be leading the pieces where they want them to go. This activity does a wonderful job of opening the door to talk with kids about how God might be leading them.

WHAT YOU'LL DO

1. Make a photocopy of the puzzle page for each child. Have kids write their names on it.

2. Have kids cut the squares apart and arrange them all upright in a square, out of order. Have kids remove one piece. Then have them slide pieces into the empty spot one at a time to arrange them in the correct order, adding in the missing piece when they're all done.

3. Lead kids in this discussion:

- **How well did you know how to lead your pieces around?**

- **Tell about someone who you trust to lead you.**

4. Read aloud Psalm 23. Lead kids in this discussion:

- **How is the way God leads us like or unlike the way you led your pieces?**

- **What are some ways God has led you?**

- **What's one area where you're not sure how God is leading you?**

5. Say: **In our psalm, David called God a shepherd. A shepherd leads sheep to water, through danger, and to green pastures so they can eat. And God leads us, too. He knows exactly where to lead us, unlike the way some of us led our puzzle pieces around. And we can be like sheep and follow him.**

6. Send the papers home with kids so they can talk with their families about the questions on their puzzle.

SOLUTION
SHOWN ON
PAGE 122

THE LORD IS MY SHEPHERD

Psalm 23

Cut apart these pictures. Then place them all faceup but in a jumbled order. Remove one piece, and slide another piece into the empty spot. Continue to slide one piece at a time into the empty spot until you've put the picture back in order, adding in the missing piece at the end.

TALK
With Your Family

▶ **In what ways is God like a shepherd who leads sheep?**

▶ **How can you follow your shepherd better?**

SOLOMON'S SEARCH FOR MEANING

Ecclesiastes 12:1-3, 13

wisdom, putting God first

Most word searches include a list of words to find. But this word search focuses even more on seeking by omitting that list! Kids will search blindly for words and by doing so will understand the pitfalls of searching for meaning without God.

WHAT YOU'LL DO

1. Make a photocopy of the puzzle page for each child. Have kids write their names on it.

2. Have kids try to find as many words as they can in the puzzle. When kids think they're done, check to see if they found all eight words.

3. Lead kids in this discussion:

- **Which words did you find that are things you've tried to get?**

- **When does chasing after "wants" become a bad thing?**

- **Why aren't any of these things enough?**

4. Say: **A man in the Bible named Solomon did a lot of searching for things like these. He looked for pleasure in work, friendship, power, money, the future, and health. But he found out that none of these things can really make us happy. Let's read about what Solomon discovered.**

5. Read aloud Ecclesiastes 12:1-3, 13. Lead kids in this discussion:

- **Why is remembering and obeying God more important than any of the things we found in our puzzle?**

- **How can you seek God above anything else?**

6. Say: **Solomon was the wisest man who ever lived. But even he tried to find pleasure in things other than God! We can learn from Solomon's example and recognize that nothing will ever satisfy us the way honoring God does.**

7. Send the papers home with kids so they can talk with their families about the questions on their puzzle.

SOLUTION
SHOWN ON
PAGE 122

SOLOMON'S SEARCH FOR MEANING

Ecclesiastes 12:1-3, 13

Look for words that are things people want. See how many you can find!

S	U	C	C	E	S	S	R	V	L
P	M	O	N	E	Y	D	O	Z	L
F	G	H	A	I	N	E	J	B	O
B	C	E	L	G	F	A	M	E	V
N	P	L	V	Q	W	B	N	S	E
P	O	P	U	L	A	R	I	T	Y
A	W	D	I	K	U	T	L	I	M
L	E	I	P	O	D	S	N	N	C
U	R	D	C	P	H	O	N	E	S
R	W	E	F	B	A	D	S	U	L

TALK
With Your Family
▶ What are some things you try to find satisfaction in?
▶ Why is seeking satisfaction through God better?

THE FIERY FURNACE

Daniel 3

standing up in faith, standing out

Preschoolers love finding items that don't fit in. But in this puzzle they'll discover that often, people who love Jesus don't fit in. Like Shadrach, Meshach, and Abednego, Christians look and act differently from those around them.

WHAT YOU'LL DO

1. Make a photocopy of the puzzle page for each child. Help kids write their names on it.

2. Have kids circle the shape or object that doesn't match the others in each row.

3. Lead kids in this discussion:

- **How could you tell which item didn't match?**

4. Say: **Each row had one thing that didn't look like the others. And people who love God don't act like other people. Let's read about some men who acted differently from everyone around them.**

5. Read aloud Daniel 3:14-18. Lead kids in this discussion:

- **Why did Shadrach, Meshach, and Abednego need to do something different from other people?**

- **What are some things people who** *don't* **love God might do?**

- **What are some ways people who** *do* **love God might act differently?**

6. Say: **When we love God, we're different from other people. We might stand out from the crowd like Shadrach, Meshach, and Abednego did. When we try to obey God when other people don't, we won't match the people around us. But we'll be making the best choice!**

7. Send the papers home with kids so they can talk with their families about the questions on their puzzle.

SOLUTION
SHOWN ON
PAGE 123

THE FIERY FURNACE

Daniel 3

Circle the items that don't match in each set.

T ALK
With Your Family

▶ **What are some things that make Christians different from other people?**

▶ **What's one way you want to be different from other people?**

DANIEL AND THE LIONS' DEN

Daniel 6

God's plan, trusting God

This puzzle is a bit more open-ended than most, and kids will love the chance to creatively express themselves. But this puzzle does more than provide a creative outlet. It lets kids talk about God's big picture for their lives—and how they can trust him no matter what that plan is.

WHAT YOU'LL DO

1. Make a photocopy of the puzzle page for each child. Have kids write their names on it.

2. Have kids draw a picture that includes the scribble on their puzzle page. Half of the kids should close their eyes while they draw; the others should keep their eyes open.

3. Have kids hold up their drawings to compare the blind ones with the sighted ones. Then discuss these questions:

- **What do you notice about the difference between the drawings of the people who could see and the people who couldn't?**

- **For those of you who had to keep your eyes closed, what was your plan for your drawing? How did it turn out?**

- **For those of you who got to keep your eyes open, what was your plan? How did your drawing turn out?**

- **Tell about a time you felt like you didn't know the whole plan for something you were doing.**

4. Read aloud Daniel 6:10-16. Lead kids in this discussion:

- **Daniel didn't know what God had planned next. He could see just the little squiggle of what was happening right then. Why might it have been tempting for Daniel to not pray?**

- **From the way Daniel behaved, what can you learn about trusting God's plan?**

5. Read aloud Daniel 6:19-23. Lead kids in this discussion:

- **Now we can see God's whole plan. How does God's plan for Daniel help *you* trust God?**

6. Say: **Daniel didn't know that God would save him from the lions. But he knew God wanted him to pray. That was the only little squiggle he could see of God's plan, but he trusted God to fill in the rest. And when God did, it was a wonderful picture! God saved Daniel from the lions! We can trust God to have good plans for us, too—even when we can see only a little piece of his plan.**

7. Send the papers home with kids so they can talk with their families about the questions on their puzzle.

NO SOLUTION SHOWN

DANIEL AND THE LIONS' DEN

Daniel 6

Turn this squiggle into a beautiful picture.

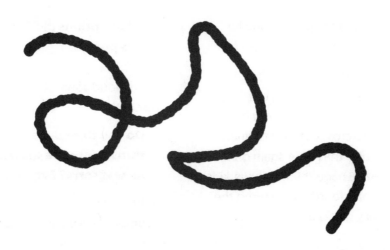

TALK
With Your Family

▶ **What's one area where you see only a small part of God's plan?**

▶ **What can you do to show that you trust God's plan?**

JONAH GETS SWALLOWED BY A FISH

Jonah 1–3

sin, repentance

Kids know the feeling of getting caught when they've disobeyed, as well as the sinking feeling of waiting to be caught! This interactive puzzle will help kids think about those feelings and why repentance is important.

WHAT YOU'LL DO

1. Make a photocopy of the puzzle page for each child. Have kids write their names on it.

2. Have kids form pairs and share a puzzle page. They'll take turns crossing out 1, 2, or 3 tally marks, with the goal of not being the one to have to cross out the last line. Then have kids play the game again on the other child's puzzle page. If time allows, kids can play a third and fourth game using the second set of tally marks on each page.

3. Lead kids in this discussion:

- **What did you do to try to avoid getting stuck with the last line?**

- **Tell about a time you knew you'd done something wrong but hadn't yet been caught. What did you do to try to avoid being caught?**

- **Describe the feelings of being caught or waiting to get caught.**

4. Read aloud Jonah 1:1-7. Say: **The sailors on the boat did something similar to our puzzle game, but it was no game for them. And Jonah got caught!**

5. Lead kids in this discussion:

- **What options did Jonah have at this point?**

6. Read aloud Jonah 1:11-15. Lead kids in this discussion:

- **Do you think Jonah's choice to be thrown into the sea truly showed that he was sorry? Explain.**

- **What are some ways you can show you're sorry when you've done something wrong?**

7. Say: **When we do something wrong, the best thing to do is repent right away. That means saying we're sorry to God and to anyone we might've hurt. Waiting to get caught—and then actually *getting* caught—is terrifying! For Jonah it was so terrifying that he told the sailors to do something that could kill him! But Jonah learned his lesson and prayed to God. Let's remember to repent when we sin.**

8. Send the papers home with kids so they can talk with their families about the questions on their puzzle.

JONAH GETS SWALLOWED BY A FISH

Jonah 1-3

Cross out 1, 2, or 3 tally marks when it's your turn. Try *not* to be the one who has to cross out the last line!

\|\|\|\|/\|\|/\|\|\|\|\|/\|\|\|\|/\|\|\|

WANNA PLAY AGAIN?

\|\|\|\|\|\|/\|\|\|\|\|\|\|/\|\|\|/\|\|

\|\|/\|\|\|\|\|\|\|\|/\|\|\|/\|\|\|/\|\|

\|\|\|/\|/\|\|\|\|/\|\|\|\|\|\|\|\|\|\|

_____

\|/\|\|\|\|\|\|\|\|\|\|\|\|/\|\|\|/\|\|\|

TALK
With Your Family

▸ Play the game again with your family!

▸ Why don't you like getting caught doing something wrong?

▸ What things do you need to repent for today?

AN ANGEL APPEARS TO MARY

Luke 1:26-38

hearing from God, understanding God's voice

Kids may be familiar with unscrambling letters to make words, but this puzzle takes that one step further. As kids make different sentences with the words provided, they'll consider how to understand God's messages for them.

WHAT YOU'LL DO

1. Make a photocopy of the puzzle page for each child. Have kids write their names on it.

2. Have kids each try to make three different sentences using the words provided. Then have kids form pairs and compare their sentences.

3. Lead kids in this discussion:

   - **How could just a few words form so many different sentences?**

   - **If you received a note from someone that was all jumbled up like this, how could you be clear about the message?**

4. Say: **In the Bible, Mary got a message from an angel that might've sounded like it was mixed up. It didn't make any sense!**

5. Read aloud Luke 1:26-38. Lead kids in this discussion:

   - **What did you notice about the way Mary tried to understand the angel's message more clearly?**

   - **What kinds of questions would you like to ask God about his messages for you?**

   - **What can you do to make sure you understand God's messages for you correctly?**

6. Say: **When there's no angel standing in front of us, it might seem like it's harder to understand God's messages to us. But we can search in the Bible or ask wise questions to make sure we know what God wants us to do. And we can respond willingly just as Mary did.**

7. Send the papers home with kids so they can talk with their families about the questions on their puzzle.

SOLUTION
SHOWN ON
PAGE 123

AN ANGEL APPEARS TO MARY

Luke 1:26-38

Use some or all of
these words to make a sentence.
Then do it again…and then again! Try to come up
with three different sentences using only the words provided.

WITHOUT

TALKING

HOW

LIVE

TO

I

AND

COULD

TO

GOD

IMAGINE

NOT

LISTENING

_____

_____

_____

_____

_____

_____

_____

TALK
With Your Family

▶ **What can you do when God's message seems confusing or jumbled up?**

▶ **What's one way you want to try to better understand God's messages to you?**

JESUS IS BORN

Luke 2:1-7

Christmas,
Jesus' birth,
celebrating Jesus

This missing-letter puzzle will start meaningful conversations about Christmas. Your kids will talk about what might be missing from their holiday celebrations, as well as how to make sure Jesus remains their focus this Christmas.

WHAT YOU'LL DO

1. Make a photocopy of the puzzle page for each child. Have kids write their names on it.

2. Have kids work individually or in pairs to add an E to each set of letters. Then have them unscramble the letters to spell a word associated with Christmas.

3. Lead kids in this discussion:

- **Which words remind you of things your family does for Christmas?**

- **Why do you like doing those things?**

4. Read aloud Luke 2:1-7. Lead kids in this discussion:

- **How ready would you say the world was for Jesus to come?**

- **What did people miss out on if they didn't make room for Jesus?**

- **In a lot of our Christmas celebrations, in what ways is Jesus like the missing E?**

- **What do you need to do to make sure your heart is ready for Christmas?**

5. Say: **A lot of times, people celebrate Christmas traditions without even thinking about Jesus. But just like the E in our puzzle, Jesus is essential for us to understand what Christmas is all about. He's the reason we celebrate! Let's make sure we make room in our hearts and our traditions for Jesus.**

6. Send the papers home with kids so they can talk with their families about the questions on their puzzle.

SOLUTION
SHOWN ON
PAGE 123

58

JESUS IS BORN

Luke 2:1-7

Each of these words is missing an E! Add an E to each set of letters, and then unscramble them to spell a word about Christmas.

 RET _____

 MRANG _____

 STERNPS _____

 VIG _____

 REDSHPH _____

 THRAW _____

 BLAST _____

 NORMANT _____

TALK
With Your Family

▶ **In which of our Christmas celebrations does Jesus seem to be missing?**

▶ **How can we make sure Jesus is the focus of all our Christmas celebrations?**

SHEPHERDS HEAR ABOUT BABY JESUS

Luke 2:8-20

Christmas, Jesus' birth, praise

With this open-ended puzzle, kids will have the opportunity to praise Jesus with the words that come to mind. Encourage kids to focus on praising Jesus.

WHAT YOU'LL DO

1. Make a photocopy of the puzzle page for each child. Have kids write their names on it.

2. Have kids find a partner and take turns playing connected words of praise.

3. Lead kids in this discussion:

- **What were some of the words you came up with?**

- **How do those words demonstrate praise?**

4. Read aloud Luke 2:8-20. Lead kids in this discussion:

- **What words would you pick to describe how the shepherds praised Jesus?**

- **Why was Jesus worthy of praise even when he was just a baby?**

- **What can you do to praise Jesus this week?**

5. Say: **The shepherds ran to see Jesus and ran to tell others about him. They knew Jesus was no ordinary baby. Jesus is worthy of our praise, too. Let's praise him this week!**

6. Send the papers home with kids so they can talk with their families about the questions on their puzzle.

SOLUTION SHOWN ON PAGE 124

60

SHEPHERDS HEAR ABOUT BABY JESUS
Luke 2:8-20

Use the letters at left to spell different words of praise to Jesus. Your words must connect to the other words you've made! Take turns with your partner, and cross out a letter when you use it. See how many words of praise you can spell!

Here are two ideas to help you get started: HOSANNA and GLORY.

A	A	A	A	A
A	B	B	C	C
C	D	D	D	E
E	E	E	E	E
F	F	G	G	H
H	I	I	I	I
I	J	K	L	L
L	L	M	M	M
N	N	N	N	O
O	O	O	O	O
P	P	P	Q	R
R	R	R	S	S
S	S	S	T	T
T	T	T	T	T
U	U	U	U	V
W	W	X	Y	Y
Y	Z			

P R A I S E

 **TALK**
With Your Family

▶ Why do these words show praise to Jesus?

▶ What actions can we do to show praise to Jesus?

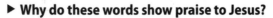

 OK TO COPY

WISE MEN VISIT BABY JESUS

Matthew 2:1-11

Christmas, looking for Jesus

The wise men followed the star to find Jesus. As kids do this puzzle, they'll follow the stars to find the answer and discuss how they can look for Jesus in their lives.

WHAT YOU'LL DO

1. Make a photocopy of the puzzle page for each child. Have kids write their names on it.

2. Have kids use one color to fill in all the squares with stars and a different color to fill in all the squares that have other shapes. Then have kids read the word that stands out.

3. Read aloud Matthew 2:1-11. Lead kids in this discussion:

   • **How did the stars help you find the word?**

   • **How did the star in the Bible help the wise men find Jesus?**

   • **What do you think of the fact that the wise men traveled so far to look for Jesus?**

   • **What helps you see Jesus at work in your life?**

4. Say: **The wise men traveled a long way because they knew the star in the sky meant someone special had been born. And when they found Jesus, they gave him expensive gifts and bowed before him. We don't have to travel to see Jesus—he's at work in our lives! Let's look for Jesus in our lives this week and worship him as the wise men did.**

5. Send the papers home with kids so they can talk with their families about the questions on their puzzle.

SOLUTION
SHOWN ON
PAGE 124

WISE MEN VISIT BABY JESUS

Matthew 2:1-11

Use one color to fill in all the stars. Use another color to fill in all the other shapes. Then see what word appears!

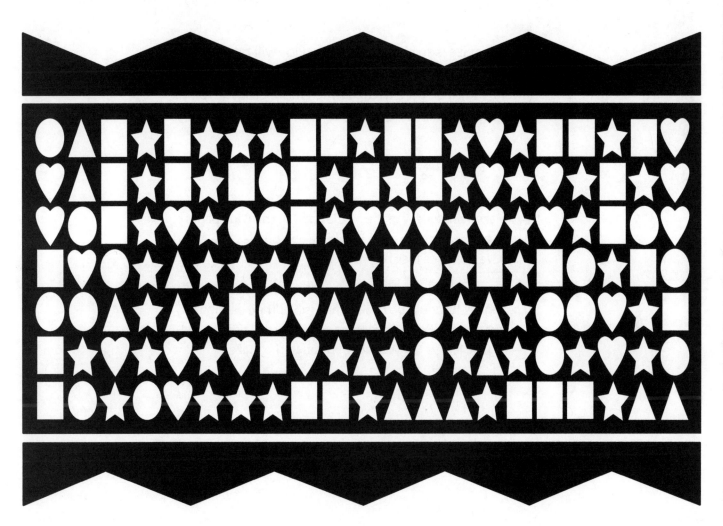

- ▶ The wise men used the star to find Jesus. What things help you see Jesus in your life?

- ▶ How can you look for Jesus at work in your life this week?

JOSEPH GOES TO EGYPT

Matthew 2:13-23

following God,
the Bible

This maze is so challenging that kids will be unlikely to finish it within the time limit. But with the guidance of the letters, they'll be able to do it much more easily! Use this puzzle to help kids know how to seek God's guidance.

WHAT YOU'LL DO

1. Make a photocopy of the puzzle pages A and B (on pages 65 and 67) for each child. Distribute *only* puzzle page A, and have kids write their names on it.

2. Give kids two minutes to try to solve the maze on puzzle page A. It should be nearly impossible. Then distribute puzzle page B and have them try again, this time following the letters to guide them through the maze.

(continued on page 66)

SOLUTION
SHOWN ON
PAGE 125

64

JOSEPH GOES TO EGYPT

Matthew 2:13-23

Try to complete this maze in two minutes or less.

A

START

END

OK TO COPY

following God,
the Bible

UPPER ELEMENTARY

WHAT YOU'LL DO NEXT

3. Lead kids in this discussion:

- **What was hard about solving the maze the first time?**

- **Do you ever wish God's plan for you was spelled out as clearly as in the second maze? Why or why not?**

4. Read aloud Matthew 2:13-23. Lead kids in this discussion:

- **How is the way God led Joseph like or unlike our second maze?**

- **How is the way God led Joseph like or unlike the way he leads us today?**

- **In what ways can the Bible be just as good as or even better than a vision like Joseph had?**

5. Say: **You might wish that God would speak to you about what to do as clearly as he spoke to Joseph. The good news is, he does! The Bible is full of God's messages to us. With or without visions from God, we can know what to do by following his Word.**

6. Send the papers home with kids so they can talk with their families about the questions on their puzzle.

SOLUTION
SHOWN ON
PAGE 125

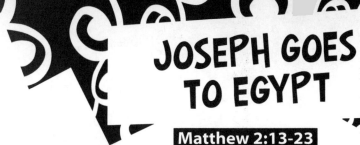

JOSEPH GOES TO EGYPT

Matthew 2:13-23

Try to complete this maze in two minutes or less.

START

END

TALK With Your Family

▶ **Which maze feels more like your life right now? Why?**

▶ **How has God's Word helped guide you in the past?**

67

OK TO COPY

JESUS AS A BOY IN THE TEMPLE

Luke 2:41-52

wisdom, God's Word

Kids love riddles, but these riddles have a purpose! They'll help kids see how impressive Jesus was to the temple teachers at even a young age.

WHAT YOU'LL DO

1. Make a photocopy of the puzzle page for each child. Have kids write their names on it.

2. Have kids try to figure out the answers to the riddles. After a few minutes, call time and see what answers kids came up with. Verify their answers using the answer key.

3. Lead kids in this discussion:

   - **What riddles or jokes have you heard that have really impressed you?**

   - **In what ways can the Bible be like a riddle?**

4. Read aloud Luke 2:42-47. Lead kids in this discussion:

   - **Tell about a time you felt like you impressed adults.**

   - **If Jesus was just a kid, how did he know so much about the Bible?**

   - **How can Jesus help you understand the Bible when it's confusing?**

5. Say: **Sometimes the Bible can feel like a riddle. It can be hard to understand! But Jesus was able to explain it when he was just a kid. And with Jesus' power in our lives, he can give us wisdom to understand the Bible.**

6. Send the papers home with kids so they can talk with their families about the questions on their puzzle.

SOLUTION SHOWN ON PAGE 126

JESUS AS A BOY IN THE TEMPLE

Luke 2:41-52

Solve the riddles, and write the answers in the blanks.

1 WHAT DO FISH LEARN IN MUSIC CLASS?

_ _ _ _ _

4 WHAT DO YOU CALL PLANTING FLOWERS BY A CHAIN-LINK FENCE?

PUTTING THE

_ _ _ _ _ _ _ _ _ _

_ _ _ _ _

2 HOW DO FISH KNOW WHEN A RACE IS OVER?

THEY REACH THE

_ _ _ _ - _ _ _ _ _ _ _ _

5 WHAT DID PETER GET WHEN HE TOOK HIS EYES OFF JESUS?

_ _ _

3 WHAT DID THE PREACHER SAY WHEN HE REALIZED HE FORGOT TO WEAR DEODORANT?

_ _ _ _

6 WHY DID THE LAMB RUN AWAY?

HE WAS FEELING

_ _ _ _ _ _ _ _ _.

TALK
With Your Family

▶ When has the Bible felt like a riddle?

▶ How can Jesus' life and teachings help you understand the rest of the Bible?

JESUS IS TEMPTED

Matthew 4:1-11

temptation,
God's Word

This unique puzzle will help kids see the consequences if Jesus had followed the path of Satan's temptation. The words themselves will be great discussion points for you to talk with kids about the punishment for sins.

WHAT YOU'LL DO

1. Make a photocopy of the puzzle page for each child. Have kids write their names on it.

2. Have kids use the clues to fill in words that will transform the first word to the final word. Only one letter will change on each line, but letters may be rearranged.

3. Lead kids in this discussion:

- **What did you notice about some of the consequences for changing the *stone* to *bread, throw* to *catch,* and *bow* to *all*?**

- **What consequences have you faced for doing wrong things?**

4. Read aloud Matthew 4:1-11. Lead kids in this discussion:

- **What did you notice about how Jesus fought temptation?**

- **Why is it important that Jesus didn't do what Satan asked?**

- **How can you better fight temptation?**

5. Say: **The words that helped us change *stone* to *bread, throw* to *catch,* and *bow* to *all* showed the consequences of giving in to temptation. Jesus had to die for us because we all give in to temptation. But we can avoid God's wrath by believing in Jesus, and we can watch out for temptation! Jesus can help us obey just as he did.**

6. Send the papers home with kids so they can talk with their families about the questions on their puzzle.

SOLUTION
SHOWN ON
PAGE 126

JESUS IS TEMPTED

Matthew 4:1-11

Satan tempted Jesus to turn stones into bread, to throw himself down and let angels catch him, and to bow to Satan to get all he could see. Change one letter at a time (rearranging the letters if needed) to make new words.

STONE

_ _ _ _ _

_ _ _ _ _

_ _ _ _ _

BREAD

when Jesus died, none of his were broken

Jesus does this to our sins

when Jesus came back to life, the angels outside his tomb wore these

THROW

_ _ _ _ _

_ _ _ _ _

CATCH

without Jesus' forgiveness, we'd face God's _ _ _ _

_ _ _ _ out for temptation! Satan is sneaky.

BOW

_ _ _

_ _ _

ALL

we've all sinned; we've broken this

how you feel when you disobey God

TALK With Your Family

▶ **What are some of the consequences for giving in to temptation?**

▶ **Tell about a temptation you struggle with. Which tactic that Jesus uses in Matthew 4:1-11 can help you fight that temptation?**

NICODEMUS ASKS ABOUT ETERNAL LIFE

John 3:1-21

eternal life, heaven

The missing letters in this puzzle spell a very important message. And they send a very important message about making sure Jesus isn't missing from our lives!

WHAT YOU'LL DO

1. Make a photocopy of the puzzle page for each child. Have kids write their names on it.

2. Have kids fill in the missing letters and then write those letters in order to spell a message.

3. Lead kids in this discussion:

- **How can you tell when Jesus is missing in someone's life?**

- **How can you tell that Jesus is here with you?**

4. Read aloud John 3:1-8. Lead kids in this discussion:

- **Would you say Jesus was missing from Nicodemus' life? Explain.**

5. Read aloud John 3:16. Lead kids in this discussion:

- **What does this verse help you understand about life with Jesus?**

- **How can you make sure that Jesus isn't missing from your life?**

6. Say: **When our verse was missing some of the letters it just didn't make much sense. And our lives don't make sense without Jesus! We need him to give us peace in this life and to help us get to heaven. God sent Jesus to save us! All we need to do is believe in Jesus, and we can live forever in heaven.**

7. Invite kids to pray with you if they'd like to acknowledge that they believe in Jesus.

8. Send the papers home with kids so they can talk with their families about the questions on their puzzle.

SOLUTION
SHOWN ON
PAGE 126

72

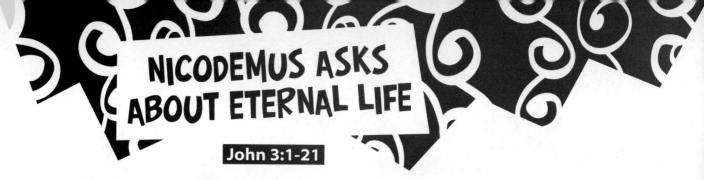

NICODEMUS ASKS ABOUT ETERNAL LIFE

John 3:1-21

Fill in the missing letters of this verse.

ohn 3:16. For God lov__d the world __o m__ch that he gave hi__ one and only Son, so that everyone who bel__eve__ in __im will not p__rish but have ete__nal lif__.

Now write the letters you added to make a sentence.

_ _ _ _ _ _ _ _ _ _ _ _ _ _ _ _ _ _ .

TALK
With Your Family

▶ **Is Jesus here in your life? When does it seem as if he's missing?**

▶ **How can you make sure you believe in Jesus?**

JESUS CALMS A STORM

worry, trusting God

Matthew 8:23-27

Kids today worry a lot. This word jumble is a great way to get kids talking about what worries them and to help them see that when life feels all mixed up, Jesus can put things back together.

WHAT YOU'LL DO

1. Make a photocopy of the puzzle page for each child. Have kids write their names on it.

2. Have kids rearrange the letters on each set of waves to form a word.

3. Lead kids in this discussion:

- **Which words are things you've personally worried about?**

- **What do you do when you're worried?**

4. Read aloud Matthew 8:23-27. Lead kids in this discussion:

- **What can you learn about worry from the way the disciples acted? from the way Jesus acted?**

- **Why can you trust Jesus with your worries?**

5. Say: **Everyone gets scared or worried sometimes. Even the disciples did, and they were grown-ups! But Jesus can calm our worries as easily as he calmed the storm. When life feels all mixed up, Jesus can put things back together. Trust Jesus with your worries!**

6. Send the papers home with kids so they can talk with their families about the questions on their puzzle.

SOLUTION SHOWN ON PAGE 126

74

JESUS CALMS A STORM

Matthew 8:23-27

The stormy waves have mixed up these words! Unscramble the letters on each set of waves to make a word.

EFUURT

FINDESR

NOYIME

VOGIMN

AHHLET

YAFILM

MOSTRS

LSCHOS

TALK
With Your Family

▶ Name one worry from the puzzle. What will you do to give that worry to Jesus this week?

▶ How can Jesus calm the worries in your life?

JESUS AND PETER WALK ON WATER

Matthew 14:22-33

focusing on Jesus, trusting God

Kids live in a world full of distractions. This puzzle will illustrate that well! They'll need to ignore the distractions—the false letters—to read the message. What a great way to talk about how to keep our eyes on Jesus!

WHAT YOU'LL DO

1. Make a photocopy of the puzzle page for each child. Have kids write their names on it.

2. Have kids read the message on the puzzle page, ignoring all the Ks, Qs, and Zs. The message comes from Matthew 28:20.

3. Lead kids in this discussion:

- **What was your strategy to not get distracted by all the extra letters?**

- **What are some things that distract you from Jesus?**

- **What's your strategy to not let those things distract you?**

4. Read aloud Matthew 14:22-33. Lead kids in this discussion:

- **What was so bad about Peter getting distracted?**

- **What benefits are there to keeping your focus on Jesus?**

- **What will you do this week to focus on Jesus?**

5. Say: **Peter had a hard time focusing on Jesus when he realized he was surrounded by wind and waves. Our fears, friends, or hobbies can threaten to take our eyes off Jesus, too. But we can stand strong and ignore those distractions and focus on Jesus.**

6. Send the papers home with kids so they can talk with their families about the questions on their puzzle.

SOLUTION
SHOWN ON
PAGE 126

76

JESUS AND PETER WALK ON WATER

Matthew 14:22-33

Ignore all the Ks, Qs, and Zs to read the message from Jesus below.

KKQZKAKQQZNZZQDKQ BKZZEZQ KZQQSKQZUZZZRQKQEZQQZ QQOQFKK

_____

ZZQKTKKHQKQIZKQSZQKZ: ZQKZKQZQKIZQKZQK ZQKZKQZKQAZKQKZQKMQKZKQZKQ

_____

ZQKZKQWQZKQKZQKZIZKQZQKTZQKZQKHZQKZKQ QKQKQZYKQKQZOKQZKQZKUZQZKQ

_____

ZQKZQKAKQKQKZLKQKZQWKQKZQKAZKQZQKKZYQKQZKQKZSQKZQKZQK,

_____

QKZQEQKZKZKVZKZKEQKZQKNZKZKZ QKZQKTZQKZQOZQKQZKQ

_____

ZQKZQKTZKQZQKHZKKZKQEKZQKZK ZKKQKZEKQKKQNKQKZKQDKQKQK

_____

ZKQKZQOKZQKFZKQKZQK ZQKZQKTKZQKZQKHQZKQKZEZQKZQK

_____

ZKQQKAZQZGKQKKEKKZQQ.

_____

TALK With Your Family

▶ What's one thing in your life that's like the Ks, Qs, and Zs—a distraction from Jesus?

▶ What can you do to better focus on Jesus?

THE TRANSFIGURATION

Matthew 17:1-9

knowing Jesus, understanding Jesus

These riddles are not as they seem! The word pictures will get kids thinking about how something can show a deeper meaning. Then kids will look at Jesus' transfiguration and consider what's so important about it—and what Jesus wants to show us about himself.

WHAT YOU'LL DO

1. Make a photocopy of the puzzle page for each child. Have kids write their names on it.

2. Have kids try to solve the five word-picture puzzles on the page, writing the meanings next to the puzzles.

3. Lead kids in this discussion:

- **How did you figure out what each word picture was trying to show you?**

- **Do you think it's clearer to show a message with a word picture or just tell what the message is? Explain.**

4. Say: **In the Bible, Jesus spent a lot of time with his disciples. One time he totally changed the way he looked to try to show them more about himself. Let's read about it.**

5. Read aloud Matthew 17:1-9. Lead kids in this discussion:

- **What can you learn about Jesus from the way he changed his appearance?**

- **What kinds of things have shown you more about who Jesus is?**

- **Do you think Jesus shows us who he is more with words or pictures? Explain.**

6. Say: **Our word pictures had a special meaning. And when Jesus changed his appearance so he glowed, he had a special meaning for the disciples. They were a little confused about the message. But we can see how powerful and amazing Jesus is by the way he was able to look like that. Jesus shows us who he is today, too. Let's keep an eye out!**

7. Send the papers home with kids so they can talk with their families about the questions on their puzzle.

SOLUTION
SHOWN ON
PAGE 126

78

THE TRANSFIGURATION

Matthew 17:1-9

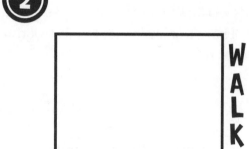 **S**olve the five word-picture puzzles, and write the meaning next to the puzzles.

1

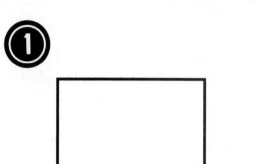

OUT

2

WALK

3

L O A D

4

T F I L

5

SPIRIT

TALK
With Your Family

▶ What's an image you have that you associate with Jesus?

▶ What has Jesus used to show you more about who he is?

 OK TO COPY

JESUS LOVES CHILDREN

Mark 10:13-16

Jesus' love,
God loves everyone

Kids will look for differences and similarities among the kids in these pictures. As they do, you'll have a great chance to talk to kids about the one thing we all have in common: Jesus loves us!

WHAT YOU'LL DO

1. Make a photocopy of the puzzle page for each child. Help kids write their names on it.

2. Have kids look for differences among the children pictured and share their observations. Then have kids look for similarities and share those.

3. Lead kids in this discussion:

- **What are some differences among those of us here?**

- **What are some things we all have in common?**

4. Say: **One thing everyone has in common is that Jesus loves us. When Jesus lived on earth, a lot of people didn't pay much attention to kids. But Jesus did!**

5. Read aloud Mark 10:13-16. Lead kids in this discussion:

- **How do you know Jesus loves you?**

- **What are some things that can make it hard for you to love someone?**

- **Why would Jesus love everyone, even people who are hard for us to love?**

6. Say: **No one is the same. We all have hair or skin that's a different color, and some of us might wear glasses while others don't. And then there are the differences that make it hard for us to love people sometimes, such as when they act mean. But Jesus loves everyone! Let's show Jesus' love to people this week.**

7. Send the papers home with kids so they can talk with their families about the questions on their puzzle.

SOLUTION
SHOWN ON
PAGE 126

JESUS LOVES CHILDREN

Mark 10:13-16

Look for differences among these children. Share your observations. Now look for similarities and share those.

TALK
With Your Family

▸ What's different about you and your friends?

▸ How do you know Jesus loves you and your friends all the same?

JESUS HEALS A BLIND MAN

Mark 10:46-52

faith,
seeing Jesus

This puzzle will get kids thinking about **common phrases** as well as what these phrases show about common understandings of **blindness**. This can help kids understand Bartimaeus better—and locate the "blind spots" in their own faith.

WHAT YOU'LL DO

1. Make a photocopy of the puzzle page for each child. Have kids write their names on it.

2. Have kids work in pairs to try to figure out each phrase containing the word *blind*.

3. Lead kids in this discussion:

- **What do these phrases demonstrate about being blind?**

- **What are some things you think would be harder to do if you were blind?**

4. Read aloud Mark 10:46-52. Lead kids in this discussion:

- **What are some things the blind man did to show he had faith?**

- **What's the connection between blindness and faith?**

- **In what ways can you show you have faith—even when you can't see what Jesus is doing?**

5. Say: **Bartimaeus showed a lot of faith. Without even being able to see Jesus, he begged for Jesus' help. And when Jesus healed him, Jesus was probably the first thing Bartimaeus could see! Bartimaeus continued to show faith by following Jesus. We can't see Jesus, and we can't always be clear on what he's up to in our lives. But we can cry out for his help and follow him, just as Bartimaeus did!**

6. Send the papers home with kids so they can talk with their families about the questions on their puzzle.

SOLUTION
SHOWN ON
PAGE 126

82

JESUS HEALS A BLIND MAN

Mark 10:46-52

The following sets of words describe phrases that include the word *blind*. Can you figure out what the phrases are?

1 IMPAIRED LIKE A WINGED NOCTURNAL CREATURE

2 SURPRISE ATTACK SOMEONE

3

4 YOU WEAR THIS WHEN YOU HIT A PIÑATA

IGNORE A SERIOUS ISSUE

BELIEVING NO MATTER WHAT

5

6

ONE UNINFORMED PERSON GUIDING ANOTHER

7

A TRIO OF VISUALLY IMPAIRED RODENTS

8

A GAME OF TAG WHERE "IT" CAN'T SEE

TALK With Your Family

▶ What's one area where you feel blind to what God is up to?

▶ How can you show faith when you feel blind like that?

JESUS HEALS A PARALYZED MAN

forgiveness, spiritual healing

Luke 5:17-26

When Jesus offered the paralyzed man forgiveness, he astounded the crowd. It seemed completely backward to those expecting healing and blasphemous to those who didn't understand who Jesus was. Kids may not have fully grasped just how backward this seemed, but elements of their own faith may seem backward. This backward puzzle is the perfect way to begin a conversation about that.

WHAT YOU'LL DO

1. Make a photocopy of the puzzle page for each child. Have kids write their names on it.

2. Have kids read the lines backward to find the word on each line. Each word is spelled backward but has no wrong letters mixed in.

3. Lead kids in this discussion:

- **How does reading backward compare with reading forward?**

- **Tell about a time something God did seemed backward to you.**

4. Say: **In the Bible, Jesus did something that seemed completely backward to the people around him. Let's read about it.**

5. Read aloud Luke 5:17-26. Lead kids in this discussion:

- **Based on the people's reactions, what seemed so backward about what Jesus did?**

- **Why is forgiveness actually more important than healing?**

- **What are some things Jesus has forgiven you for?**

6. Say: **The Pharisees thought it was backward for Jesus to offer forgiveness at all. They didn't think anyone but God could do that! But what** *they* **had backward was not understanding that Jesus** *is* **God. And Jesus knew that forgiveness was a more important priority than a man being able to walk. We can experience Jesus' forgiveness, too!**

7. Send the papers home with kids so they can talk with their families about the questions on their puzzle.

SOLUTION
SHOWN ON
PAGE 126

84

JESUS HEALS A PARALYZED MAN

Luke 5:17-26

Hidden in each line of letters is a word spelled backward. Can you find each word? (Hint: Each word can be found in Luke 5:17-26.)

GEDNEVIGROFEB _____

OGNILAEHFREM _____

IRFAHTIAFEEHC _____

DEDEZYLARAPOY _____

EBUODWORCER _____

EZIRDESIARPAMA _____

TALK With Your Family

▶ **Why might free forgiveness seem backward to some people today?**

▶ **Why is forgiveness really the most important thing?**

THE GOOD SAMARITAN

kindness, helping others

Luke 10:30-37

As kids put their logic skills to work with this puzzle, they'll also think about what excuses they've made to avoid helping others and how they can love their neighbors the way Jesus taught.

WHAT YOU'LL DO

1. Make a photocopy of the puzzle page for each child. Have kids write their names on it.

2. Have kids use the clues to solve the logic puzzle. As they eliminate answers, they'll put an X in that box. When they have the correct answer, they'll put an O.

3. Lead kids in this discussion:

- **Which risks on our chart seem like the most important to consider? Why?**

- **What are some risks you've taken to help someone?**

4. Say: **The answers in our puzzle come from a story Jesus told about helping and loving others.**

5. Read aloud Luke 10:30-37. Lead kids in this discussion:

- **How would you describe the point of Jesus' story?**

- **What are some ways you're good at helping people?**

- **Why is it important to help others, even if we have to make personal sacrifices?**

6. Say: **The priest wouldn't have been able to do his job if he'd touched an injured man because the Bible had laws about what made a priest "unclean." He would've had to go through cleansing rituals and wait until he was clean again. The temple assistant may have feared for his safety—after all, one man had already been beaten and robbed! But the Samaritan didn't care about what he'd have to sacrifice. That's the way God wants us to love and help other people.**

7. Send the papers home with kids so they can talk with their families about the questions on their puzzle.

SOLUTION SHOWN ON PAGE 127

THE GOOD SAMARITAN

Luke 10:30-37

A man was robbed and left for dead on a busy road. Three people saw him, had to consider different risks, and reacted in different ways. Use the clues in the box at right to determine who did what.

Use the grid below to cross-reference each option with the other categories. Mark pairs you know aren't true with an X, and mark pairs you know are related with an O. If you know, for example, that the priest wasn't concerned about safety, you can add an X in the box where the priest column and safety row meet. If you knew those two were related, you'd mark that box with an O. Do this after each clue, and eventually you'll have filled in enough Xs and Os that you can use process of elimination to finish the puzzle.

1. The person whose main risk was safety wasn't the Samaritan.
2. The person who stopped to help was either the one who would risk money and cultural differences or the priest.
3. The priest didn't look at the man and then pass by.
4. The temple assistant didn't have to risk shame or uncleanness.
5. The temple assistant did look at the man but didn't stop to help.
6. The priest's main concern wasn't safety.
7. The Samaritan didn't pass by the man.

		priest	temple assistant	Samaritan	stopped to help	looked at man, passed by	passed by
R I S K	safety	X					
	money, cultural differences						
	shame, uncleanness						
A C T I O N	stopped to help						
	looked at man, passed by						
	passed by						

TALK
With Your Family

▶ What excuses have you made to not help someone?
▶ What's one thing you can do this week to help someone?

OK TO COPY

THE LOST SHEEP AND COIN

Luke 15:3-10

salvation,
God's kingdom

LOWER ELEMENTARY

Fill-in puzzles like this one are all about putting things in their place. Jesus' point in the lost sheep and coin parables had a similar message: We all have a place in God's kingdom, and he'll search for us to put us in that place. Use this puzzle as a kind of parable to help kids see the value and place we each have in God's kingdom.

WHAT YOU'LL DO

1. Make a photocopy of the puzzle page for each child. Have kids write their names on it.

2. Have kids find the right place in the puzzle for all the words on the list.

3. Lead kids in this discussion:

   • **How did you find out where each word went?**

   • **Tell about a time you misplaced something. Why did you want it back in the right place?**

4. Read aloud Luke 15:3-10. Lead kids in this discussion:

   • **Tell about a time you got lost. Why was it important that someone find you?**

   • **What does Jesus mean when he compares people with important things someone lost?**

   • **What do you think about the idea that God has a special place for you in his kingdom?**

5. Say: **The shepherd looked for his lost sheep, and the woman looked for her lost coin—because they were important! These people wanted the sheep and coin back in the right place. In the same way, we're important to God and he'll look for us so we can find our place in heaven.**

6. Send the papers home with kids so they can talk with their families about the questions on their puzzle.

SOLUTION
SHOWN ON
PAGE 127

88

THE LOST SHEEP AND COIN

Luke 15:3-10

When the shepherd lost his sheep and the woman lost her coin, they looked all over so they could put them back in the right place. Put these words in the right place by seeing where they fit into our puzzle. (Hint: Count the letters!)

JOY
LOST
SHEEP

FOUND
COINS
SWEEP

REJOICE
SEARCH
STRAYED

TALK
With Your Family

▶ What are some things you have a special place for?

▶ What does it mean to you that God has a special place for you?

OK TO COPY

JESUS AND ZACCHAEUS

repentance, transformation

Luke 19:1-10

Kids will have to do some counting to solve this puzzle—and counting was a regular part of Zacchaeus' job as a tax collector. Best of all, they'll consider how Zacchaeus counted things differently when Jesus changed his life!

WHAT YOU'LL DO

1. Make a photocopy of the puzzle page for each child. Have kids write their names on it.

2. Have kids fill the numbers 1 through 4 into the puzzle so each row has one of each number, each column has one of each number, and each box has one of each number.

3. Lead kids in this discussion:

- **What made this puzzle easy or difficult for you?**

- **What did you do to make sure you had all the right numbers?**

4. Say: **Zacchaeus was a man in the Bible whose job was math. He collected tax money from people. But he purposely did the math wrong to get extra money for himself! Then Zacchaeus met Jesus.**

5. Read aloud Luke 19:1-10. Lead kids in this discussion:

- **What was different about Zacchaeus' math after he met Jesus?**

- **What does that show about how Jesus changed Zacchaeus' heart?**

- **What are some ways Jesus has changed your heart?**

6. Say: **After Zacchaeus met Jesus, he knew he couldn't live the same way, so he changed. That's called** *repentance.* **When we spend time with Jesus, we'll want to repent from doing the wrong thing and do the right thing instead. That's because Jesus changes us!**

7. Send the papers home with kids so they can talk with their families about the questions on their puzzle.

SOLUTION
SHOWN ON
PAGE 128

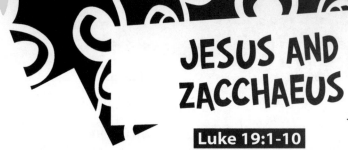

JESUS AND ZACCHAEUS

Luke 19:1-10

Fill in the numbers 1 through 4 so each row, column, and box has one of each number.

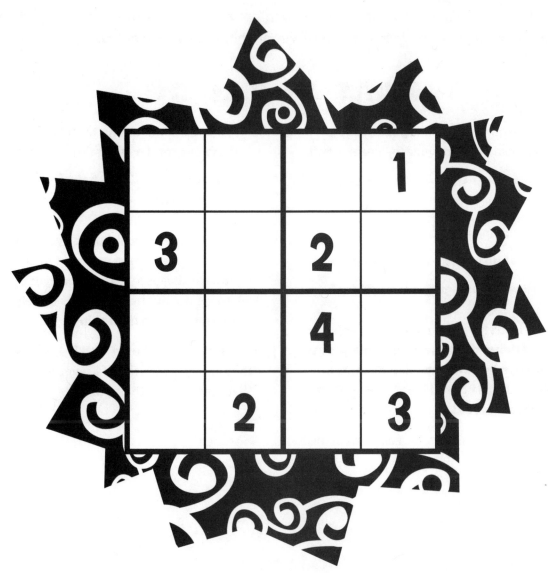

TALK
With Your Family

▶ What was so bad about Zacchaeus' math before he met Jesus?

▶ What can you learn from the way Zacchaeus changed after he met Jesus?

OK TO COPY

THE WOMAN AT THE WELL

John 4:4-30

repentance, growing relationship with God

Kids will enjoy figuring out the patterns in this puzzle. But you can also challenge them to think about patterns of sin in their lives—wrong things they keep doing.

WHAT YOU'LL DO

1. Make a photocopy of the puzzle page for each child. Help kids write their names on it.

2. Have kids determine and draw the next shape in each pattern.

3. Lead kids in this discussion:

- **What do you like about patterns?**

- **How do you figure out a pattern?**

4. Say: **Jesus met a woman in the Bible who kept doing the same wrong things over and over again. It was like a pattern. When Jesus figured it out, this is what the woman said.**

5. Read aloud John 4:19-24. Lead kids in this discussion:

- **What are some wrong things you've done over and over again?**

- **What can Jesus do to change that pattern?**

6. Say: **Jesus doesn't want us to keep doing the same wrong thing over and over again. He always loves and forgives us when we do, but he also wants to help us learn to do the right thing.**

7. Send the papers home with kids so they can talk with their families about the questions on their puzzle.

SOLUTION SHOWN ON PAGE 128

WILDLY CREATIVE PUZZLES WITH A POINT

Figure out what shape comes next in each pattern. Then draw it!

TALK
With Your Family

▶ What's a pattern?

▶ How can doing the wrong thing over and over again be like a pattern?

93

JESUS FEEDS 5,000

John 6:1-13

provision, gifts from God

To kids, this puzzle will seem as if it has no end! Just when they think they've made all the words they can, they'll find another one. This provides a great illustration about how God keeps on giving to us and providing for our needs.

WHAT YOU'LL DO

1. Make a photocopy of the puzzle page for each child. Have kids write their names on it.

2. Have kids use the letters provided to make as many words as they can in five minutes. Then have kids find a partner and see if their partner made any words they missed.

3. Lead kids in this discussion:

- **How complete do you think your list is?**

- **How many words do you think can be made out of these 15 letters?** (Get ready to wow kids: The answer is 4,988 English words!)

- **How can just 15 letters make so many different words?**

4. Read aloud John 6:1-13. Lead kids in this discussion:

- **Jesus took a few pieces of food and made enough for everyone. How do you think he did that?**

- **When has God amazed you with more than you needed?**

- **What's a basic need of life that you know you really don't need to worry about having enough of?**

5. Say: **The letters in our puzzle kept making more and more words. That's kind of like what Jesus did with the bread and fish—he made a lot from a little. But in Jesus' case, that was a miracle. Every day, God does miracles in our lives by providing us with enough food, clothes, and love. God provides more than we need!**

6. Send the papers home with kids so they can talk with their families about the questions on their puzzle.

SOLUTION
SHOWN ON
PAGE 128

JESUS FEEDS 5,000

John 6:1-13

Make as many words as you can think of using some or all of these letters. You can use the same letters over and over to make new words.

A B C D E G I L N N O S T T Y

_____ _____ _____

_____ _____ _____

_____ _____ _____

_____ _____ _____

_____ _____ _____

_____ _____ _____

_____ _____ _____

_____ _____ _____

TALK With Your Family

▸ In what ways has God given you way more than you need?

▸ What's one area where you feel like you want God to provide more?

JESUS' TRIUMPHANT ENTRY

Mark 11:1-11

praise, worship

Preschoolers love drawing, and they'll enjoy adding their finishing touches to this incomplete picture. Don't worry about the quality of their coloring; instead, let kids draw freely and share about how they can use everything they have to worship Jesus.

WHAT YOU'LL DO

1. Make a photocopy of the puzzle page for each child. Help kids write their names on it.

2. Have kids add lines to the picture to complete the drawing. They may also color it in, if time allows.

3. Lead kids in this discussion:

- **What was wrong with the picture when you first got it?**

- **What's so silly about a picture not being finished?**

4. Read aloud Mark 11:1-11. Lead kids in this discussion:

- **The people in Jerusalem praised Jesus with everything they had. What are some things you can use to praise Jesus?**

- **Jesus doesn't want us to praise him unless we really mean it all the way. How can you tell you really want to praise Jesus?**

5. Say: **When we praise Jesus but don't really mean it, it's kind of like the way our picture started out. It's not finished! Jesus wants us to praise him and mean it in our hearts. We can praise Jesus all the time, anywhere!**

6. Send the papers home with kids so they can talk with their families about the questions on their puzzle.

SOLUTION
SHOWN ON
PAGE 129

96

JESUS' TRIUMPHANT ENTRY

Mark 11:1-11

This picture of Jesus on Palm Sunday isn't finished! Can you finish it?

TALK
With Your Family

▸ How can you praise Jesus all the time?

▸ Why is it important to always praise Jesus?

L
O
W
E
R

E
L
E
M
E
N
T
A
R
Y

THE LAST SUPPER

communion, Jesus' death

Matthew 26:17-30; John 13:1-11

This matching puzzle may seem a bit simple for lower-elementary kids, but the discussion that goes with it is what will help kids really understand the symbols of Jesus' death—and what his death means for them.

WHAT YOU'LL DO

1. Make a photocopy of the puzzle page for each child. Have kids write their names on it.

2. Have kids draw lines to connect each symbol with its meaning.

3. Read aloud John 13:3-10. Lead kids in this discussion:

- **Why did Jesus wash the disciples' feet?**

- **Why do you think one of the last things Jesus did with his disciples was serve them?**

4. Read aloud Matthew 26:20-25. Lead kids in this discussion:

- **What's the meaning of the bowl?**

- **How can you stay true to Jesus?**

5. Read aloud Matthew 26:26. Lead kids in this discussion:

- **What's the meaning of the bread?**

- **Why did Jesus have to die?**

6. Read aloud Matthew 26:27-29. Lead kids in this discussion:

- **What's the meaning of the cup?**

- **Why does Jesus' blood represent forgiveness?**

- **Why do you need Jesus' forgiveness?**

7. Say: **At his last supper with the disciples, Jesus used a lot of symbols to help the disciples understand what was going to happen. The symbols he used were all common things they'd see so they'd have regular reminders of what Jesus did for them. We can also remember that Jesus died for us and offers us forgiveness.**

8. Send the papers home with kids so they can talk with their families about the questions on their puzzle.

SOLUTION
SHOWN ON
PAGE 129

THE LAST SUPPER

Matthew 26:17-30; John 13:1-11

Jesus used different symbols to remind the disciples of different things. Match each symbol with its meaning.

JESUS' DEATH AND BODY

SERVICE

JESUS' BLOOD AND FORGIVENESS

BETRAYING JESUS

TALK
With Your Family

▶ Which symbol stands out to you the most? Why?

▶ What other things remind you of Jesus' death and forgiveness?

JESUS DIES

Mark 15:16-39

Jesus' death, forgiveness

This is a word search with a twist: It's not fair! Kids are very familiar with things seeming unfair, and this word search will bring up those feelings. Use this puzzle to help kids talk about whether Jesus' death for everyone—no matter how bad they are—really seems fair.

WHAT YOU'LL DO

1. Make a photocopy of the puzzle page for each child. On half of the puzzles, cut off the right side where the word list is.

2. Have kids try to complete the word search by finding all the words. Don't offer any clues or help the kids who don't have the list. Provide enough time so everyone with the list finds all the words, and then call time.

3. Lead kids in this discussion:

- **What was unfair about this puzzle?**

- **How do you react when things are unfair?**

4. Read aloud Mark 15:27-32. Lead kids in this discussion:

- **What was unfair in these verses about the way Jesus was treated?**

- **What do you think about Jesus doing that for you?**

5. Read aloud Mark 15:33-39. Lead kids in this discussion:

- **What was unfair in these verses about the way Jesus was treated?**

- **Why does it matter that the Son of God died like a criminal?**

6. Read aloud Romans 3:23-24. Lead kids in this discussion:

- **What do you think about the idea that *anyone* can receive Jesus' forgiveness—even people who've done more bad things than you? Is that fair? Explain.**

7. Say: **Jesus' death on the cross wasn't fair to him. He had never done anything wrong, but he died like a criminal. He chose to do that because he loves everyone so much. Sometimes it might not seem fair that people who have done really bad things can be forgiven just as easily as people who haven't done such bad things. But Jesus' love isn't like our puzzle—everyone gets the same shot! We can all receive Jesus' forgiveness, no matter what we've done wrong.**

8. Send the papers home with kids so they can talk with their families about the questions on their puzzle.

SOLUTION SHOWN ON PAGE 129

JESUS DIES

Mark 15:16-39

Find the words hidden in this puzzle.

E	R	P	N	W	O	R	C	C	G
R	A	G	E	N	I	V	E	H	S
B	L	V	O	M	F	S	V	I	S
E	S	A	C	R	I	F	I	C	E
L	W	D	T	E	L	K	G	N	N
I	E	R	E	E	T	S	R	D	K
E	N	S	P	K	S	P	O	E	R
V	I	E	R	O	C	M	F	A	A
E	S	L	R	A	N	O	R	T	D
O	H	C	I	M	L	I	M	H	E

DEATH

CROWN

MOCKED

CROSS

BELIEVE

FORGIVE

VINEGAR

SACRIFICE

SIN

DARKNESS

TALK
With Your Family

▶ **What seems fair or unfair about your own forgiveness?**

▶ **Tell about someone you don't really think deserves forgiveness. What do you think about the idea that Jesus died for that person too?**

JESUS COMES BACK TO LIFE

Luke 24:1-12

salvation, Jesus' resurrection

Kids may be a little frustrated as they do this word search because not all the words are actually hidden. Stop the puzzle before kids get too frustrated, and help them see that Jesus conquered death—and our sins are gone!

WHAT YOU'LL DO

1. Make a photocopy of the puzzle page for each child. Have kids write their names on it.

2. Have kids try to complete the word search by finding all the words. Allow enough time for kids to find many of the words, but stop when they seem frustrated that they can't find some of the words. The words *sin*, *death*, *liar*, *cheater*, and *disobey* are missing from the puzzle.

3. Lead kids in this discussion:

- **What did you notice about the words you couldn't find in the puzzle?**

4. Read aloud Luke 24:1-12. Lead kids in this discussion:

- **How do our missing words tie into Jesus' resurrection?**

- **What did Jesus' resurrection mean for the women and Peter, who found his tomb empty?**

- **What does Jesus' resurrection mean for us?**

5. Read aloud Romans 6:6-9. Lead kids in this discussion:

- **How do you know if sin and death no longer have power over your life?**

- **If Jesus' death took away sin's power, why do people who believe in Jesus still sin?**

6. Say: **Our puzzle was missing the words *sin*, *death*, *liar*, *cheater*, and *disobey* because Jesus' resurrection means sin and death have lost their power. The Bible says we can be alive with Jesus, and those words no longer have power over our lives. God sees us through the lens of Jesus now—and we're forgiven!**

7. Send the papers home with kids so they can talk with their families about the questions on their puzzle.

SOLUTION
SHOWN ON
PAGE 130

JESUS COMES BACK TO LIFE

Luke 24:1-12

Find the words hidden in this puzzle.

DEATH   FORGIVEN   HOLY   HEAVEN

LIFE   CHEATER   SIN   DISOBEY

VICTORY   PERFECT   ALIVE   RISEN

LIAR

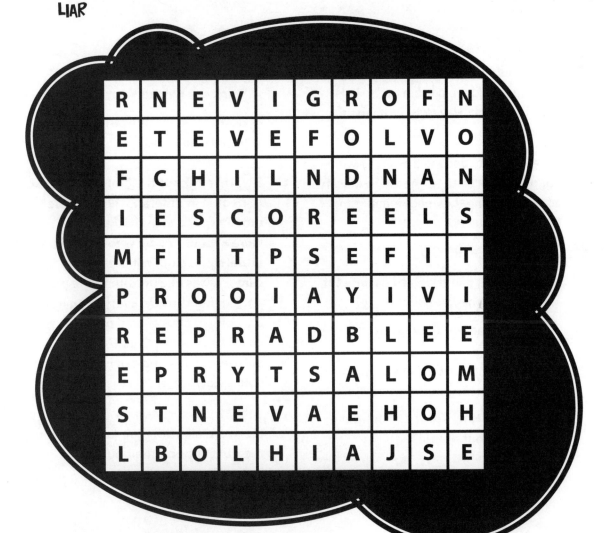

R	N	E	V	I	G	R	O	F	N
E	T	E	V	E	F	O	L	V	O
F	C	H	I	L	N	D	N	A	N
I	E	S	C	O	R	E	E	L	S
M	F	I	T	P	S	E	F	I	T
P	R	O	O	I	A	Y	I	V	I
R	E	P	R	A	D	B	L	E	E
E	P	R	Y	T	S	A	L	O	M
S	T	N	E	V	A	E	H	O	H
L	B	O	L	H	I	A	J	S	E

TALK
With Your Family

▶ **What does Jesus' death and resurrection mean for you personally?**

▶ **How can your life be different if you believe in Jesus?**

OK TO COPY

THE HOLY SPIRIT COMES

Acts 2:1-6

understanding God, relying on the Holy Spirit

When the Holy Spirit came, it was like the ultimate decoder for people to understand God. People heard God's message in their own language, and new doors were opened up for everyone to understand who God is. Kids will get to experience that firsthand as they attempt to do this puzzle with and without the key.

WHAT YOU'LL DO

1. Make a photocopy of the puzzle page for each child. Fold the bottom half so kids can't see the key. Have kids write their names on it.

2. Have kids try to decode the puzzle without peeking at the key. Then have kids try again, unfolding their papers and using the key as a guide.

3. Lead kids in this discussion:

- **What was it like trying to decode the puzzle before you had the key?**

- **Why was the key so helpful?**

4. Read aloud Acts 2:1-6. Lead kids in this discussion:

- **How is the Holy Spirit like or unlike the key to our puzzle?**

- **Why is it important that the Holy Spirit can help us know God better?**

- **How can the Holy Spirit help you understand God?**

5. Say: **Throughout the Bible, God spoke to people in different ways. But he mostly spoke to individuals, and there were a lot of people who didn't know or understand God. When the Holy Spirit came, it was like unfolding the puzzle and seeing the key. Everything became a whole lot clearer, and now everyone could hear about God! The Holy Spirit is still here today and can help us understand God better.**

6. Send the papers home with kids so they can talk with their families about the questions on their puzzle.

SOLUTION SHOWN ON PAGE 130

104

THE HOLY SPIRIT COMES

Acts 2:1-6

Decode this puzzle.

"✔♥))✳) ■♥▼ ♠✗★✗✪✚ ✳▼ ▼♥
_____

➤➤♠✗★✳♥◆▲ ✔✗■✗♠✪▼✳♥■▲, ➤◆▼ ■♥●
_____

➤✖ (✳▲ ▲➤➤✳♠✳▼ (✗ (✪▲ ♠✗★✗✪✚✗) ✳▼
_____

▼♥ (✳▲ (♥✚✖ ✪➤➤♥▲▼✚✗▲ ✪■)
_____

➤➤♠♥➤➤(✗▼▲." — ✗➤➤(✗▲✳✪■▲ ❖:✸
_____

(Decoded: "GOD DID NOT REVEAL IT TO PREVIOUS GENERATIONS, BUT NOW BY HIS SPIRIT HE HAS REVEALED IT TO HIS HOLY APOSTLES AND PROPHETS." — EPHESIANS 3:5)

KEY

A	B	C	D	E	F	G	H	I	J	K	L	M
✪	➤	◖	)	✗	❮	✔	◗	✳	⬠	✳	✚	◆

N	O	P	Q	R	S	T	U	V	W	X	Y	Z
■	♥	➤➤	✦	♠	▲	▼	◆	★	●	◐	✖	❰

0	1	2	3	4	5	6	7	8	9
❀	✲	✳	❖	✺	✸	☆	✿	❄	❅

TALK
With Your Family

▶ How can the Holy Spirit help us understand God?

▶ What's different between the way people heard from God in the Old Testament and the way people do now?

PETER AND JOHN HEAL A LAME MAN

Acts 3:1-10

helping others, kindness

Kids are familiar with Peter and John's dilemma. They often don't have much money to give people. This puzzle will help kids think about what they *do* have to offer people: Jesus' love and kindness.

WHAT YOU'LL DO

1. Make a photocopy of the puzzle page for each child. Have kids write their names on it.

2. Have kids cut out the coins in each row and then tape them back in the correct order to form words.

3. Lead kids in this discussion:

- **Why are the actions described by the words you unscrambled even better than just giving people money?**

- **What are some things people need that money can't buy?**

4. Read aloud Acts 3:1-10. Lead kids in this discussion:

- **The man was begging for money. What did he really need?**

- **What can you learn from the way Peter and John helped the man even though they had no money?**

- **What's one act of kindness you can do for someone else this week?**

5. Say: **People often help other people by giving money to charities. And that's a good thing! But it's not the only way to help people. Peter and John didn't have any money, but they were able to offer this man the love of Jesus! We can do the same thing. The way we rearranged our coins made a whole list of ways to help people, and those ways of helping are even more valuable than money.**

6. Send the papers home with kids so they can talk with their families about the questions on their puzzle.

SOLUTION
SHOWN ON
PAGE 130

106

PETER AND JOHN HEAL A LAME MAN

Acts 3:1-10

Cut out one row of coins at a time. Rearrange the letters, and then tape them in the correct order to spell a word that's something we can do for other people. Then write letters on the blank coins to spell another thing you can do for someone else.

E V L O

S K I N S E N D

S E J U S

S W D O R

P H L E

P S E C T E R

○ ○ ○ ○ ○ ○ ○ ○

OK TO COPY

TALK With Your Family

▶ Which set of coins spells out something you'd like to do for someone else?

▶ How can you do it?

SAUL'S BLINDING LIGHT

Acts 9:1-9

transformation, growing relationship with God

Kids are growing and changing physically, mentally, and spiritually all the time. But they may not realize they can be intentional about growing with Jesus. This puzzle will help kids see how God took the old Saul and made him new—and he can do the same for us.

WHAT YOU'LL DO

1. Make a photocopy of the puzzle page for each child. Have kids write their names on it.

2. Have kids think of ways to change the word OLD to NEW one letter at a time. Kids who finish early may try to think of other ways to change it, as there are several possible answers.

3. Lead kids in this discussion:

- **When have you seen someone take something old and use it for something new?**

4. Read aloud Acts 9:1-9. Lead kids in this discussion:

- **What were some of the ways Jesus changed Saul's life and made it new?**

5. Read aloud 2 Corinthians 5:17. Lead kids in this discussion:

- **What in your life was old—before Jesus—or makes you think of life without him? How has Jesus made you new?**

- **How do you need Jesus to keep on changing you?**

6. Say: **Jesus changed Saul from someone who tracked down and hurt Christians to someone who loved Jesus and told everyone about him. What a change! No wonder he wrote that Jesus makes us new creations. And the more we get to know Jesus, the more he'll keep changing the old to new.**

7. Send the papers home with kids so they can talk with their families about the questions on their puzzle.

SOLUTION SHOWN ON PAGE 130

108

SAUL'S BLINDING LIGHT

Acts 9:1-9

Change one letter at a time to change the word OLD to NEW. You can also move letters to new spots each turn. For example, if you were trying to change MEAN to PAUL you could change MEAN to LEAN, PLAN, PAUL. Try to find different ways to do it!

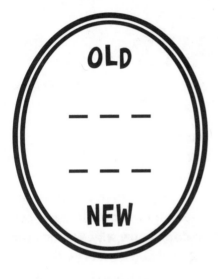

OLD
_ _ _
_ _ _
NEW

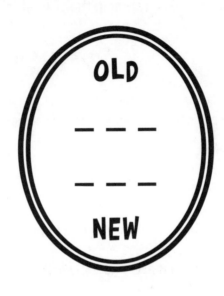

OLD
_ _ _
_ _ _
NEW

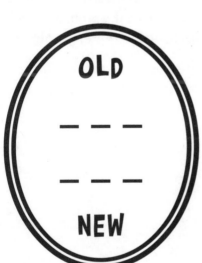

OLD
_ _ _
_ _ _
NEW

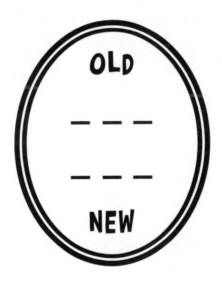

OLD
_ _ _
_ _ _
NEW

TALK
With Your Family

▶ Tell about some people you've seen Jesus change from old to new.

▶ What old things in your life might Jesus want to make new?

PETER'S PRISON ESCAPE

Acts 12:6-11

rescue, prayer

Lower-elementary kids will love solving this maze. They are learning to pray, so thinking about how God can help them in difficult times will be a wonderful fruit of this puzzle.

WHAT YOU'LL DO

1. Make a photocopy of the puzzle page for each child. Have kids write their names on it.

2. Have kids try to get out from the center of the maze.

3. Lead kids in this discussion:

- **What's bad about being in prison?**

4. Read aloud Acts 12:6-11. Lead kids in this discussion:

- **Think about the way God helped Peter. How can God help you?**

- **What's something you want to pray about right now?**

5. Lead kids in prayer for the things they share. Have kids hold their fingers on the center of the maze during the prayer and move them to the outside when you finish praying.

6. Say: **Peter was in prison for telling people about Jesus. He had done good things but was in a bad place. Sometimes we get punished and we deserve it. But sometimes bad things happen and we don't know why. We can always talk to God when we feel like bad things are happening. He can help us feel better or help make the problem go away, just like he helped Peter get out of jail.**

7. Send the papers home with kids so they can talk with their families about the questions on their puzzle.

SOLUTION
SHOWN ON
PAGE 131

PETER'S PRISON ESCAPE

Acts 12:6-11

Peter is stuck in jail!
Can you get him out?

TALK
With Your Family

▶ What's something bad that's happened to you?

▶ How can praying to God help you when bad things happen?

JESUS WILL COME BACK

Revelation 22

heaven, eternal life

This puzzle is shaped like a circle—a symbol that life with Jesus is never-ending. As kids identify the promises about heaven from this circle, they'll see that eternal life has already begun and will never end.

WHAT YOU'LL DO

1. Make a photocopy of the puzzle page for each child. Have kids write their names on it.

2. Have kids try to identify the two sentences about heaven by reading every other letter.

3. Lead kids in this discussion:

- **What excites you about these promises?**

4. Read aloud Revelation 22:3-5. Lead kids in this discussion:

- **What things are broken about life right now?**

- **What perfect things are you excited about in heaven?**

5. Read aloud Revelation 22:12-13. Lead kids in this discussion:

- **What does it mean that Jesus is the beginning and the end?**

- **What questions do you have about eternity?**

- **How can you celebrate that life with Jesus has already begun?**

6. Say: **Jesus has no beginning and no end. He always has been and always will be. When Jesus comes back and takes us to heaven, we'll experience eternal life in a perfect place! If we believe in Jesus, we know we'll go to heaven. And even though we live in a broken world right now, we can enjoy the fact that our forever relationship with Jesus is already happening!**

7. Send the papers home with kids so they can talk with their families about the questions on their puzzle.

SOLUTION SHOWN ON PAGE 131

JESUS WILL COME BACK

Revelation 22

Jesus is forever—the
A and Z, the beginning and the end.
This circle has two promises about heaven, and they
alternate letters. Figure out where each promise begins and what it says.

PERAERPSANROIDNEGAATPHLNAECVEEFROSRIUCSKJNEOSMUOSRIEST

TALK
With Your Family

▶ What excites you about heaven?

▶ If you're alive when Jesus comes back, what do you want to be doing?

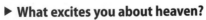

OK TO COPY

God Creates the World

SOLUTION TO PUZZLE ON PG. 9

You Are Special

SOLUTION TO PUZZLE ON PG. 11

no window lines, number changed on jersey, stripe on side of jersey changed, bench changed color, girl's wristband switched wrists, basketball rotated

Adam and Eve's Bad Choice

SOLUTION TO PUZZLE ON PG. 13

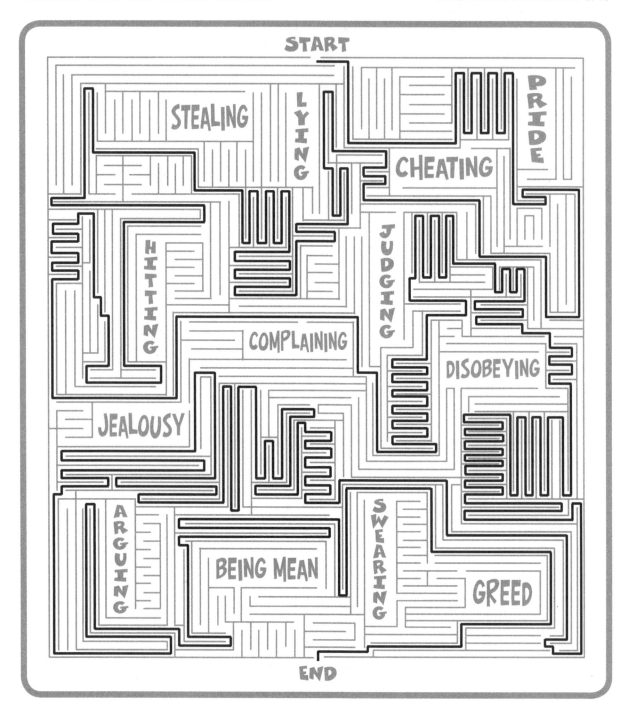

Noah and the Flood

SOLUTION TO PUZZLE ON PG. 15

Rabbits A and F; Elephants C and F

Joseph's Rainbow Coat

1–D, 2–C, 3–B, 4–A

SOLUTION TO PUZZLE ON PG. 17

God Protects Baby Moses

SOLUTION TO PUZZLE ON PG. 19

Moses and the Burning Bush

God is calling you.

SOLUTION TO PUZZLE ON PG. 21

G						O		D	I
S									
	C				A				
		L							
		L							
I							N		
									G
Y							O		U

The Ten Plagues

SOLUTION TO PUZZLE ON PG. 23

locusts, frogs, flies, livestock, lightning

God Parts the Red Sea

SOLUTION TO PUZZLE ON PG. 25

power, timing, safety, mighty, trust

The Ten Commandments

SOLUTION TO PUZZLE ON PG. 27

Love your neighbor (Bible); Rest one day a week (Ten Commandments); Don't steal (Ten Commandments); Take care of creation (Bible); Obey your parents (Ten Commandments); Look both ways before crossing (not in Bible); Don't lie (Ten Commandments); Wash your hands before dinner (not in Bible); Don't be jealous (Ten Commandments); Go to church every Sunday (not in Bible); Don't kill (Ten Commandments); Drink plenty of water (not in Bible); Put God first (Ten Commandments); Respect other people (Bible); Pray for your enemies (Bible); Only talk to Christians (not in Bible); Don't worship idols (Ten Commandments); Respect God's name (Ten Commandments)

Jericho's Falling Walls

SOLUTION TO PUZZLE ON PG. 29

hope, trust, faith, joy, love, peace

Ruth Stays With Naomi

SOLUTION TO PUZZLE ON PG. 31

dog and bone, lamp and lightbulb, mailbox and letter, sock and sock, banana and monkey, game board and game pawn

Samuel Hears God

SOLUTION TO PUZZLE ON PG. 33

Be still, and know that I am God! (Psalm 46:10)

Samuel Anoints David

SOLUTION TO PUZZLE ON PG. 35

David Kills Goliath

SOLUTION TO PUZZLE ON PG. 37

KINDNESS, HOPE, LOVE, JUSTICE, BRAVERY, HONOR, TRUST, PEACE, INTEGRITY, JOY, COURAGE, FAITH, PATIENCE

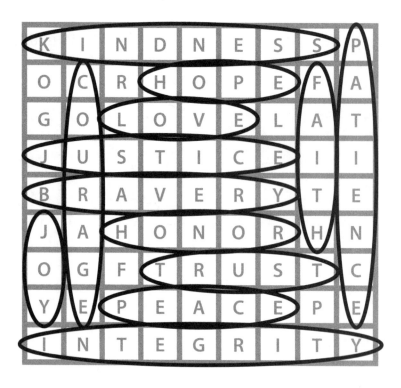

Solomon Asks for Wisdom

SOLUTION TO PUZZLE ON PG. 39

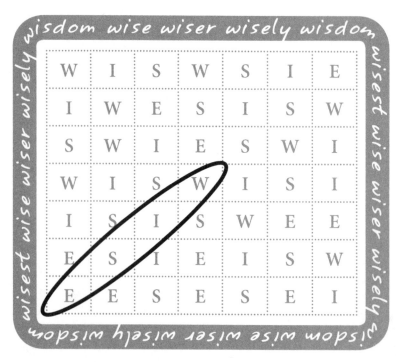

Ravens Feed Elijah

SOLUTION TO PUZZLE ON PG. 41

Across: FRIENDS, HOME, TOYS, LOVE, AIR
Down: FAMILY, CASH, WATER, CLOTHES, FOOD

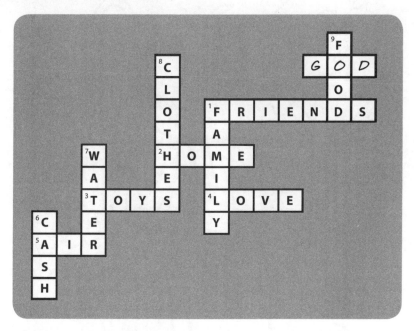

Elijah and the Prophets of Baal

SOLUTION TO PUZZLE ON PG. 43

drought, famine, prophets, danced, Lord, shouted, stones, fire, altar, water

King Josiah Cleans the Temple

SOLUTION TO PUZZLE ON PG. 45

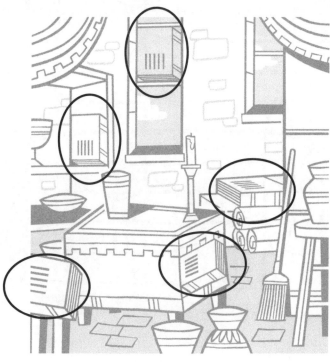

The Lord Is My Shepherd

SOLUTION TO PUZZLE ON PG. 47

Solomon's Search for Meaning

SOLUTION TO PUZZLE ON PG. 49

Possible answers: SUCCESS, MONEY, FAME, POPULARITY, IPODS, PHONES, POWER, LOVE

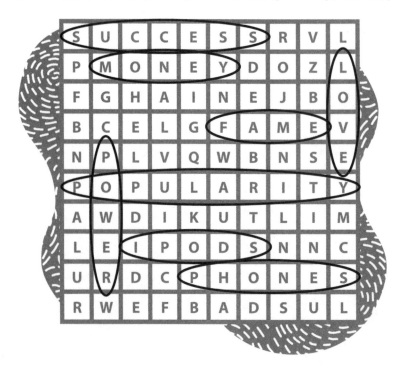

The Fiery Furnace

SOLUTION TO PUZZLE ON PG. 51

Daniel and the Lions' Den

SOLUTION TO PUZZLE ON PG. 53

No solution necessary.

Jonah Gets Swallowed By a Fish

SOLUTION TO PUZZLE ON PG. 55

No solution necessary.

An Angel Appears to Mary

SOLUTION TO PUZZLE ON PG. 57

Possible sentences (kids may come up with others): I could not imagine how to live without talking and listening to God; I could not imagine talking to God; God and I could not live; I could live without talking and listening to God; I could imagine how to live not talking and listening to God; I live talking without listening to God.

Jesus Is Born

SOLUTION TO PUZZLE ON PG. 59

tree, manger, presents, give, shepherd, wreath, stable, ornament

Shepherds Hear About Baby Jesus

SOLUTION TO PUZZLE ON PG. 61

Possible answers:

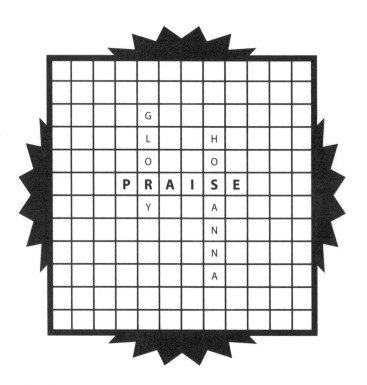

Wise Men Visit Baby Jesus

SOLUTION TO PUZZLE ON PG. 63

JESUS

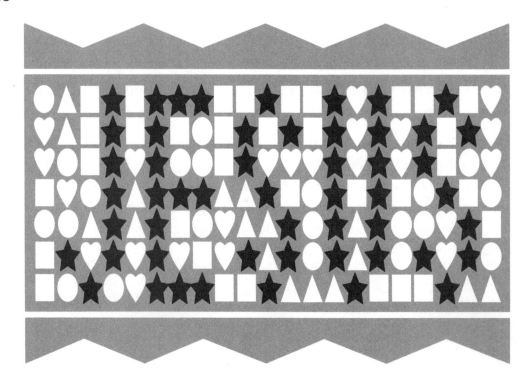

Joseph Goes to Egypt

SOLUTION TO PUZZLE ON PG. 67

START

END

Jesus as a Boy in the Temple

SOLUTION TO PUZZLE ON PG. 69

1) scales; 2) fin-ish line; 3) pew; 4) petal to the metal; 5) wet; 6) sheepish

Jesus Is Tempted

SOLUTION TO PUZZLE ON PG. 71

stone–bones, bones–robes, robes–bears, bears–bread
throw–wrath, wrath–watch, watch–catch
bow–low, low–law, law–all

Nicodemus Asks About Eternal Life

SOLUTION TO PUZZLE ON PG. 73

Jesus is here.

Jesus Calms a Storm

SOLUTION TO PUZZLE ON PG. 75

money, health, school, friends, family, storms, moving, future

Jesus and Peter Walk on Water

SOLUTION TO PUZZLE ON PG. 77

And be sure of this: I am with you always, even to the end of the age.

The Transfiguration

SOLUTION TO PUZZLE ON PG. 79

1) out of the box; 2) sidewalk; 3) wide load; 4) uplift; 5) Holy Spirit

Jesus Loves Children

SOLUTION TO PUZZLE ON PG. 81

Various responses.

Jesus Heals a Blind Man

SOLUTION TO PUZZLE ON PG. 83

1) blind as a bat; 2) blindside; 3) turn a blind eye; 4) blindfold; 5) blind faith; 6) the blind leading the blind; 7) blind man's bluff; 8) Three Blind Mice

Jesus Heals a Paralyzed Man

SOLUTION TO PUZZLE ON PG. 85

forgiven, healing, faith, paralyzed, crowd, praised

The Good Samaritan

SOLUTION TO PUZZLE ON PG. 87

Person	Action	Main Risk
priest	passed by	shame, uncleanness
temple assistant	went to look at man, passed by	safety
Samaritan	stopped to help	money, cultural differences

		priest	temple assistant	Samaritan	stopped to help	looked at man, passed by	passed by
R I S K	safety	X	O	X	X	O	X
	money, cultural differences	X	X	O	O	O	O
	shame, uncleanness	O	X	X	X	X	O
A C T I O N	stopped to help	X	X	O			
	looked at man, passed by	X	O	X			
	passed by	O	X	X			

The Lost Sheep and Coin

SOLUTION TO PUZZLE ON PG. 89

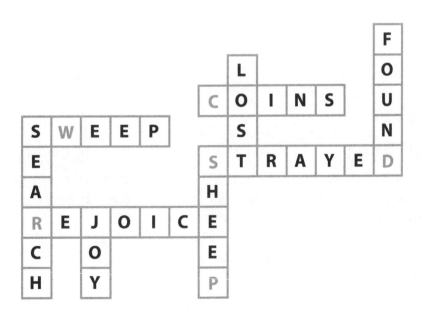

Jesus and Zacchaeus   *SOLUTION TO PUZZLE ON PG. 91*

2	4	3	1
3	1	2	4
1	3	4	2
4	2	1	3

The Woman at the Well   *SOLUTION TO PUZZLE ON PG. 93*

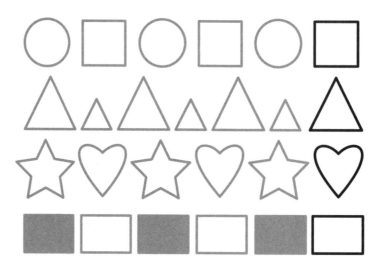

Jesus Feeds 5,000   *SOLUTION TO PUZZLE ON PG. 95*

Possible words include: toes, tones, stone, stony, God, dog, bad, bade, tons, notes, not, ton, cab, base, bait, baits, loan, loans, bone, bones, cone, cones, balding, bending, tending, lending, leaning, and many more!

128

Jesus' Triumphant Entry

SOLUTION TO PUZZLE ON PG. 97

The Last Supper

SOLUTION TO PUZZLE ON PG. 99

bowl—betraying Jesus; bread—Jesus' death and body; washing foot—service;
cup—Jesus' blood and forgiveness

Jesus Dies

SOLUTION TO PUZZLE ON PG. 101

CROWN, VINEGAR, SACRIFICE, BELIEVES, SIN, MOCKED, CROSS, FORGIVE, DEATH,
DARKNESS

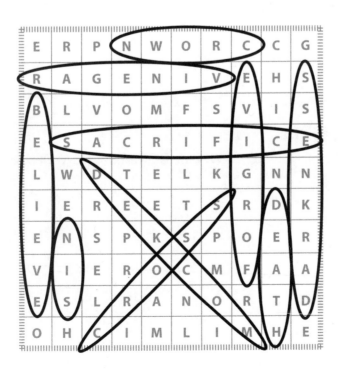

Jesus Comes Back to Life

SOLUTION TO PUZZLE ON PG. 103

Words not in puzzle: death, liar, cheater, sin, disobey

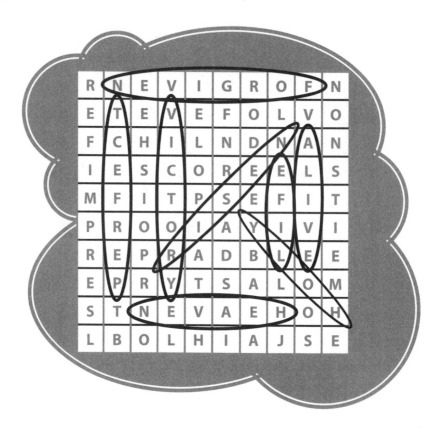

The Holy Spirit Comes

SOLUTION TO PUZZLE ON PG. 105

"God did not reveal it to previous generations, but now by his Spirit he has revealed it to his holy apostles and prophets." – Ephesians 3:5

Peter and John Heal a Lame Man

SOLUTION TO PUZZLE ON PG. 107

love, kindness, Jesus, words, help, respect

Saul's Blinding Light

SOLUTION TO PUZZLE ON PG. 109

Possible solutions: OLD, ODE, WED, NEW; OLD, DON, WON, NEW; OLD, LOW, NOW, NEW

Peter's Prison Escape

SOLUTION TO PUZZLE ON PG. 111

Jesus Will Come Back

SOLUTION TO PUZZLE ON PG. 113

Jesus is preparing a place for us; no more tears, no death, never sick.

INDEX BY SCRIPTURE
OLD TESTAMENT

NEW TESTAMENT

INDEX BY FAITH-BUILDING THEME

INDEX BY AGE

PRESCHOOL

LOWER ELEMENTARY

UPPER & LOWER ELEMENTARY

UPPER ELEMENTARY

Tons of fun ways to reinforce Bible points!

The Humongous Book of Games for Children's Ministry

Super-size fun with 220 games that reinforce Bible points. You'll always have a great big fun game at your fingertips for any area of children's ministry. Indexed by Scripture and energy level.

► ISBN 978-0-7644-2355-0
  $29.99 *In Canada $32.99*

Also available in this series:

The Humongous Book of Bible Skits

► ISBN 978-0-7644-3083-1 • $29.99
  In Canada $32.99 (BOOK & CD)

The Humongous Book of Children's Messages

► ISBN 978-0-7644-2647-6 • $29.99
  In Canada $32.99

The Humongous Book of Preschool Ideas

► ISBN 978-0-7644-3601-7 • $29.99
  In Canada $32.99

The Humongous Book of Preschool Ideas 2

► ISBN 978-0-7644-3813-4 • $29.99
  In Canada $32.99

Order today! Visit group.com or your favorite Christian retailer.

Secret weapons for *getting kids' attention!*

Throw & Tell® Balls

Group's Throw & Tell Balls get—and keep—kids' attention when you finish a lesson early, kids show up grumpy, or you need an icebreaker—fast! Simply inflate a sturdy, colorful ball and let kids toss the ball around for a few seconds. When you call "Time," the child holding the ball reads what's written under his or her left thumb—and then everyone answers (or the child answers, depending on how you choose to play). Kids love the Throw & Tell Balls, and you'll love seeing them open up, laugh, and connect with one another in this new way.

NOTE: *All balls inflate to 24" diameter. Comes in hangable bag.*

THROW & TELL BALLS   *For age 3+ only*

[A] ATTENTION-GRABBER THROW & TELL BALL *for Children's Ministry*
Perfect for grabbing kids' attention, then launching your lessons!
▶ ISBN 978-1-4707-2031-5 • $9.99 *In Canada $10.99*

[B] PRAYER THROW & TELL BALL *for Children's Ministry*
53 prayer prompts help kids learn more about poverty.
▶ ISBN 978-1-4707-2032-2 • $9.99 *In Canada $10.99*

[C] ALL ABOUT ME THROW & TELL BALL *for Children's Ministry*
Encourage kids to learn about each other and find common connections!
▶ ISBN 978-1-4707-2033-9 • $9.99 *In Canada $10.99*

[D] THIS…OR THAT? THROW & TELL BALL *for Preteen Ministry*
Keep kids on the edge of their seats with this hilarious ball of fully loaded questions.
▶ ISBN 978-1-4707-2034-6 • $9.99 *In Canada $10.99*

[E] PRESCHOOL THROW & TELL BALL *for Preschool Ministry*
It's fun. It's super-easy. It's bouncy. And it's GUARANTEED to get your preschoolers to open up and interact!
▶ ISBN 978-0-7644-7613-6 • $9.99 *In Canada $10.99*

[F] LIFE-APPLICATION THROW & TELL BALL *for Children's Ministry*
Dozens of instant application activities!
▶ ISBN 978-1-4707-2030-8 • $9.99 *In Canada $10.99*

I teach our 3rd - 5th grade Sunday school class and also our pre-k second hour class. I used this for both classes and the kids had a blast answering the questions about themselves and learning about their friends.

—*Children's Ministry Leader, Lawton, OK*

Order today! Visit group.com or your favorite Christian retailer.

Get kids into the Bible!

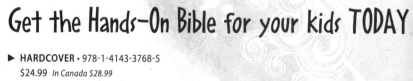